BUILDING
GIANT EARTHMOVERS

ERIC C. ORLEMANN

MBI Publishing Company

First published in 2000 by MBI Publishing Company, 729 Prospect Avenue, PO Box 1, Osceola, WI 54020-0001 USA

MBI Publishing Company books are also available at discounts in bulk quantity for industrial or sales-promotional use. For details write to Special Sales Manager at Motorbooks International Wholesalers & Distributors, 729 Prospect Avenue, PO Box 1, Osceola, WI 54020-0001 USA.

Library of Congress Cataloging-in-Publication Data
Orlemann, Eric
    Building giant earthmovers / Eric C. Orlemann.
        p. cm.— (ColorTech)
    Includes index
    ISBN 0-7603-0640-0 (pbk. : alk. paper)
        1. Mining machinery. 2. Earthmoving machinery.
    3. Excavating machinery. I. Title. II. ColorTech

TN345.O74 2000
622'.028–dc21   00-058384

On the front cover: On the front cover: At this point, the O&K RH400 is almost complete. The hydraulic cylinders from the boom to the stick still need to be connected, as does the bucket. The scale of the machine is certainly impressive when viewed from any angle. Height to the top of the tracks is 9 feet, 4 inches. *Syncrude Canada*

On the frontispiece: Behind the massive radiator housing of Terex Mining's 360-ton capacity Unit Rig MT-5500, beats the heart of a big 16-cylinder, four-cycle, quad-turbocharged Detroit Diesel/MTU 16V4000 engine, capable of mustering 2,800 gross horsepower. *Eric C. Orlemann*

On the title page: This massive LeTourneau L-1800 wheel loader, pictured at the Eagle Butte Mine, north of Gillette, Wyoming, in 1995, was the first prototype machine of the model line to be put into service. It is equipped with a substantial 45-cubic-yard combo bucket, which is designed for loading coal and overburden material. *Eric C. Orlemann*

On the back cover: The rear view of the Unit Rig MT-5500 shows off the truck's massive rear width, which measures 29 feet, 8 inches across. Tires are big 55/80R63 radials, mounted on 63-inch diameter rims. Note the design of the General Atomics/PCS retarding, forced-air grid system mounted on the upper right side of the deck. Its radial design and compact proportions follow from the company's extensive work in rail transit engines and operating systems. *Eric C. Orlemann*

Edited by Paul Johnson
Designed by Arthur Durkee

Printed in China

CONTENTS

ACKNOWLEDGMENTS

When I first took on this project, I suspected it would be one of my most challenging book endeavors to date. I was right. The act of catching some of the largest machines ever made in various stages of assembly required a bit of luck, a lot of planning, and a creative approach. Since some of the largest creations never reach final assembly until delivered to a work site, sometimes only individual components and sub-assemblies can be photographed. In some cases, special photography was provided by the manufacturers to meet my specific requirements. In others, unlimited access to film these magnificent creations as they were literally born on the plant assembly floor was granted. If it were not for the gracious help of the following individuals and companies, this undertaking would have been all but impossible.

I thank Mike Colar, Albert Yang, Pat Murphy, and Robert Johnson of Komatsu Mining Systems; Carl Volz and Sharon Holling of Caterpillar, Inc.; Larry Vargus, Peter Ahrenkiel, Bill Mateychuk, and Volker Börnke of Terex Mining; Martha Glasgow of LeTourneau, Inc.; Merilee S. Hunt of Liebherr Mining Equipment Company; Bill Williams, Ed Ward, and Mark Dietz of P&H Mining Equipment; James Rosso of Bucyrus International; Greg Halinda of Syncrude Canada, Ltd.; Nance Dania of Central Ohio Coal Company; Christine Taylor of the Peabody Group; and Ted Shehinski of Fort McMurray, Alberta, Canada.

I also thank friend and fellow author Keith Haddock for helping in the research of many long forgotten facts and for keeping me moving ever forward.

And last, I express my sincerest thanks to the many mining employees, both current and retired, of Central Ohio Coal Company and Peabody Coal who helped fill in the missing pieces of information concerning the BE 3850-B shovels and Big Muskie.

—Eric C. Orlemann

INTRODUCTION

In the world of heavy construction machinery, the sight of the many leviathans that toil in the mining industry never ceases to amaze and astound. Outside of the shipbuilding industry, the giants of the mining industry are some of the largest and heaviest mobile land machines ever built by man.

Today's modern mining giants are built using all of the available state-of-the-art computer design software and machine tool technology. Though many of these machines are built on assembly lines, they are not built at the same pace or quantity as automobiles. One might imagine hundreds of builders climbing all over these behemoths, assembling them as they continue down a massive assembly line, like worker bees attending to the queen's needs. But in reality, most of these creations are never completed until they reach their final mine site destinations. In fact, some machines are built and shipped in component modules. As they stand by themselves, these parts are difficult to recognize as part of a gigantic piece of earthmoving equipment. This was especially true with the Goliaths of the industry, the stripping shovels and walking draglines.

Since most of these colossal beasts work in rural isolated areas, the uninformed don't realize the amazing amount of work these machines have performed. Some have worked just below ground level, hiding their true scale, hidden behind walls of solid earth and rock. Seeing them on the pages of this book is difficult enough. Seeing how these incredible machines came into being is even harder to imagine. It is fascinating to see just how some of these earthmovers were designed, machined, assembled, shipped, and erected, all without letting most know of their true intent in life . . . to provide us with the necessary raw materials for sustaining our modern way of life. These miraculous machines have dug, scraped, and hauled coal, copper, iron, gold, and, yes, even diamonds. Our modern society, with all of its ups and downs, needs large volumes of raw materials to keep it ever moving forward. And mining machines, on a scale to match the monumental tasks at hand, are the only way to obtain these raw materials.

Contained within these pages are some of the most technologically advanced and largest examples of modern mining equipment in production today. Most of these creations contain state-of-the-art technology for their particular designs and functions. The equipment showcased represents a cross-section of some of the most recognizable machine categories—haulers, loaders, and shovels. We have all seen earthmoving equipment that looks very similar to the machines pictured but not quite in such earth-shattering scale. Also discussed are two bygone giant types from the 1960s: the Bucyrus-Erie 3850-B stripping shovels and the one-and-only Bucyrus-Erie 4250-W Big Muskie walking dragline. These metal monsters are simply some of the largest single-bucket earthmoving machines built in the twentieth century. Only the modern German-built bucket wheel excavators in the 240,000-cubic-meter daily output range are of equal or greater in size.

PRIME MOVERS
THE ULTRA-HAULERS

It seems as if the basic dump truck has been with us forever. In fact, the modern off-highway design concept dates back to the late 1920s. Mack, with its legendary Bulldog line of trucks, introduced its limited production AP haulers for use in the building of Boulder Dam, today known as Hoover Dam. These sturdy chain-drive trucks were the first attempt at building an off-highway type of hauler that could handle heavy loads on less-than-ideal unpaved road surfaces. Yet these trucks were little more than beefed up over-the-road designs.

The introduction of the first Euclid rear-dump truck of early 1934 marked a turning point in the manufacture of off-highway haulers. Built by the Euclid Road Machinery Company of Cleveland, Ohio, the Euclid Model Z Trac-Truk was the industry's first true off-highway hauler designed and built from the ground up for that purpose. It was also the first to utilize a simple planetary gear rear differential axle. This was a far better design than the chain-driven trucks manufacturers were

building at the time. The industry quickly recognized Euclid as a pioneer in the production of quarry and mining trucks. It was a distinction the company would hold for years to come.

Over the years haulers became more sophisticated with the introduction of automatic transmissions and more powerful diesel engines. The legendary LeTourneau-Westinghouse LW-30 Haulpak, introduced in 1957, marked the next turning point for the design of the rear-dump truck. The LW-30 was a 30-ton hauler powered by an eight-cylinder Cummins diesel engine. Key innovative design features included Hydrair air-hydraulic suspension system, sloping dump box, and left-mounted off-set cab. In the coming years, all of these features would become standard on quarry and mining trucks worldwide.

Another key innovation taking place at this time was R. G. LeTourneau's development of its TR-60, the industry's first diesel-electric-drive hauler to use traction wheel motors. The one and only TR-60 was built in 1959 and

The giant MT-5500, with its 360-ton capacity, is the third such mining truck ever to attain this lofty load limit. Officially dedicated in April 2000, it started full operations at the Jacobs Ranch Coal Mine, near Wright, Wyoming, in June 2000.

Introduced in 1974, the General Motors Terex 33-19 Titan hauler was heralded as the world's largest-capacity truck. With its 350-ton payload capacity, 3,300 gross horsepower, and 3,000 flywheel horsepower, it was without equal. But the king would have to give up its crown in 1998, when the first prototype 360-ton-capacity Caterpillar 797 and Liebherr T-282 haulers were introduced. *ECO collection*

electric-drive hauler available to the world mining market.

Over the decades, there has always been a demand for larger haulers from the mining industry. The more you can haul, the more productive and profitable your operation. If anything has delayed the introduction of big trucks, it usually has had to do with suitable powerplants and tires. Bigger payloads require greater horsepower and bigger tires. The quest for more power has led manufacturers to investigate various engine layout alternatives, such as large diesel locomotive and turbine powerplants. Along with these experimental efforts, traditional higher-revving and

The first LeTourneau-Westinghouse LW-30 "Haulpak" truck is pictured in December 1956. Conceived by Ralph Kress, this mechanical-drive, 30-ton capacity hauler would set the design criteria for off-highway mining trucks for years to come. Many of the truck's innovations are still present on today's giants, such as a sloping dump body and left-mounted offset operator's cab. *ECO Collection*

went into service in 1960. Other manufacturers would soon follow LeTourneau's lead with diesel-electric-drive designs of their own. Unit Rig & Equipment Company of Tulsa, Oklahoma, built its first experimental diesel-electric-drive hauler, known as the Lectra Haul M-64, in January 1960. The M-64 used an articulated steering frame and was the first to use General Electric traction motors mounted within the rim assemblies. Even though the truck broke in two during operational testing, the electric GE wheel motors proved their worth. In 1963, Unit Rig released its rigid-frame Lectra Haul M-85. This truck model is considered the first "full" production diesel-

Though many of the large structures on the Komatsu 930E-2 are welded by automated welding machines, a highly trained human welder is still the preferred method for the detail work, especially in tight places.

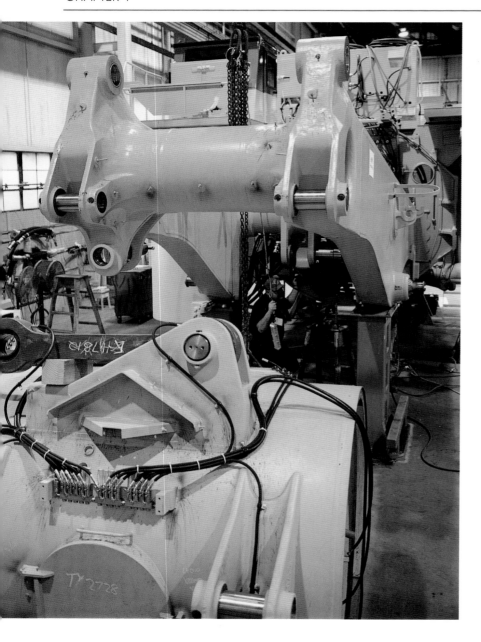

Shown from the rear, a Komatsu 930E-2's rear axle housing is being prepared to be mounted onto the lower section of the rear frame. The housing's main function is to support the massive wheel motors and rim assemblies. Since the system is diesel-electric, there are no gears in the housing itself, which is hollow. A rear service hatch allows entry into the housing for easy maintenance of the rear drive assembly.

lighter-weight diesel engines were given steady doses of increased horsepower. Cummins, Detroit Diesel/MTU, and Caterpillar all make heavy-duty diesels with power ratings suitable for today's big haulers.

Manufacturers have also experimented with the number of axles on their haulers. To get maximum payloads, tandem-drive designs have been tried many times, with mixed results. In their favor, tandem-drive haulers can take greater payloads than single-drive axle designs. They can also use slightly smaller tires, which are more cost-effective in theory—though they use more of them. On the down side, tandem-drive layouts cost more and present some very unpleasant handling characteristics, such as extreme understeer in some working situations. There's nothing scarier for a truck driver than a fully loaded tandem-drive hauler that won't turn when the steering wheel is turned, when he's heading down a steep grade, toward a curve, in the wet. On paper, the tandem-drive haulers make perfect sense. But in reality, their higher operating costs made mining owners stick to the tried-and-true two-axle, single-drive, six-tire layout.

Quite often mining equipment manufacturers have to wait for tire technology to catch up with their designs. It's easier to make a larger machine than to create a tire capable of withstanding the extra stresses such a vehicle produces under load. The two industries have a push-pull relationship. As the tire manufacturers introduce a larger tire, the truck builders increase their capacities, which, in turn, creates demand for still larger tires. This one-upmanship continues even today, with no end in sight.

The 930E-2 has two engine choices—the Detroit Diesel/MTU 16V4000, or in this case, the Cummins Quantum QSK60. The QSK60 shown being installed here is a 16-cylinder, four-cycle, two-stage intercooled and aftercooled quad-turbocharged diesel, rated at 2,700 gross horsepower and 2,550 flywheel horsepower at 1,900 rpm. Dry weight of the engine alone is 19,515 pounds. Front radiator core is an L&M Mesabi split-flow, with a capacity of 157 gallons.

Once the main sections of a 930E-2 truck are assembled, they are partially disassembled for the final coat of factory paint. This unit has just emerged from the paint booth and is undergoing final preparations for shipping. The final delivery assembly depends on the mode of transport, truck or rail. More of the front end structures can be left on for rail transport. These structures would have to be removed if shipped by semitruck and trailer, because of width restrictions.

As suitable engines and tires became available, mining haulers continued to grow in size. In the 1970s, fleets with capacities of 150 to 170 tons dotted the world mining map. The 1980s would see trucks with 190- to 240-ton capacities become the haulers of choice. The 1990s were dominated in part by the 240-ton class, with the odd 250- to 260-ton fleet in use at some mines. This time period also saw the birth of a new hauler class, the mighty ultra-hauler.

The ultra-hauler represents the pinnacle of efficient, heavy-duty mining trucks. These trucks feature a two-axle design with six tires. Drivetrain layout is either diesel-electric or mechanical. But most important is capacity. The ultra-hauler class includes trucks with a capacity rating of 300 tons and above. Yes, the Terex 33-19 Titan hauler from 1974 was a 350-ton giant. But its one-of-a-kind status, plus its three-axle, tandem-drive layout put it in different era of monster trucks. The ultra-haulers are simply the most technologically advanced heavy-duty mining trucks in the world.

Except for Caterpillars, all ultra-haulers make use of a diesel-electric powertrain using state-of-the-art AC traction drive systems. Before the introduction in 1995 of the Komatsu 930E, with its revolutionary GE-designed AC drive system, all haulers with this drivetrain layout made do with DC traction motors. The AC systems, originally developed for use in high-horsepower diesel locomotives, offered the mining industry drive components that are far more efficient than comparable DC designs. AC drive offers improved retarding capabilities for braking; slip and slide control in low-traction situations; reduced maintenance and repair costs, which reduce downtime; and the ability to achieve higher haulage speeds with greater control. Several manufacturers now make AC drive systems. In fact, each of the first three builders of this type of truck uses an AC drive system from a different supplier. And then there's Caterpillar, which has never given up on the mechanical drivetrain.

Komatsu 930E

The Komatsu 930E Haulpak of 1995 was the first true, two-axle, 300-ton-plus ultra-hauler to make it into

Here, a worker connects one of the main air intake lines of a 930E-2 from the front-mounted air cleaners to the engine bay area. At this stage in the manufacturing process, the final coat of paint has already been applied.

full production. However, BelAZ Trucks of the Republic of Belarus built a two-axle, 308-ton-capacity hauler identified as the Model 75501 in 1991, but it was strictly a one-off prototype for field testing and evaluation. Its 310-ton capacity, General Electric AC drive, and big 48/95R57 tires made it state of the art upon introduction. The 930E comes from a long line of Haulpak trucks, dating back to the very first one in 1957—the LW-30. Since that time, the truck line has carried the names

This 930E, pictured in 1998, was the 100th unit of this type built. Shown while awaiting delivery by rail from the Komatsu Peoria assembly plant in Illinois, it would eventually find a home in the Powder River Basin at the Black Thunder Mine in Wright, Wyoming. The tires and dump body for this unit were shipped directly from other manufacturers to the mine site to reduce transportation costs.

of LeTourneau-Westinghouse, WABCO, and Dresser. In 1988, Komatsu, Ltd., of Japan and Dresser Industries of Dallas, Texas, formed a 50/50 joint venture company known as Komatsu Dresser Company (KDC) for the purpose of building construction and mining equipment in the Western Hemisphere. By 1995, Komatsu had gained 100 percent ownership of the company. Since 1997, Haulpak trucks have been sold under the Komatsu Mining Systems, Inc. banner.

All of Komatsu's big mining trucks are built in Peoria, Illinois, at the same location where R. G. LeTourneau first set up shop in the state in 1935. The 930E was a natural outgrowth of the company's long-running and very popular 240-ton class hauler, the 830E. Not long after the 830E hit the ground in 1988, it became the world's most popular diesel-electric, 240-ton-capacity truck. The leading-edge technology and manufacturing techniques that made the 830E such a stellar performer would also go into the big 930E. While the 830E utilized the industry-accepted standard DC electrical drive layout, the 930E was designed around new AC drive technology from day one. Codeveloped by General Electric and Komatsu, it was the first hauler of any kind to use the AC drive system. The benefits of AC drive, as well as the truck's high technology and manufacturing standards, made the 930E an instant success.

In developing the 930E's box-sectional frame, one of the single most important components in a haul truck, engineers applied the most advanced computer-aided design, finite element analysis, and full dynamic and static testing. Steel castings at all critical stress transition zones make the truck's frame one of the strongest in the industry. The frame features integral roll-over protective structure (ROPS) supports, integrated front bumper, rear tubular cross-members, and a rugged, continuous horse collar. All Komatsu mining truck frames are fabricated and tested at the Peoria facilities.

The first few 930E haulers were powered by the Detroit Diesel/MTU 16V396 TB44L, four-cycle, 16-cylin-

This is what it's all about. A big Komatsu 930E takes on 80 tons of rock and earth per shovel cycle. After four passes, the truck is ready to roll with 320 tons on its back. Gross vehicle weight of the 930E fully loaded is 1,100,000 pounds. *Komatsu Mining System*

der engine, rated at 2,682 gross horsepower and 2,500 flywheel horsepower. In 1997, the Detroit Diesel/MTU 16V4000, four-cycle, 16-cylinder engine became the engine of choice. It produced a similar power output of 2,700 gross horsepower and 2,500 flywheel horsepower. With the new engine came an increase in payload capacity, which was bumped up to 320 tons.

The tires on the 930E were specially designed by Bridgestone to handle the massive hauler's tremendous payloads. The 48/95R57 VELS radial tires were 12.5 feet in diameter, with each tire rated at carrying 80 tons. At the

17

These are the massive front wheel assemblies for the Liebherr T-282. The ball-joints connect to two front suspension parallel control arms, attached to a single, massive nitrogen-oil cylinder per side, giving the truck top performance in the handling and turn radius departments.

time of this tire's introduction in 1995, it was the world's largest off-highway radial truck tire.

It takes weeks to build a behemoth like the 930E, beginning with small teams who start with the bare frame. When the main engine assembly, rear axle housing, and upper decking have been installed, the structure is transported to the paint booth on the opposite side of the diesel-electric drive assembly plant. The main structure and subassemblies are painted, and final preparation for delivery begins. Since

the 930E is not delivered as a completed unit, it is not fully assembled at the plant. Components are crated for delivery, by rail car or flat-bed truck, to the customer's mine site. Critical components supplied by outside suppliers, such as the GE AC drive wheel motors and the massive tires, are shipped directly from the manufacturer to the mine site, saving both time and transportation charges.

Once at the mine site, the 930E goes together in a matter of days. The truck is given a complete on-site

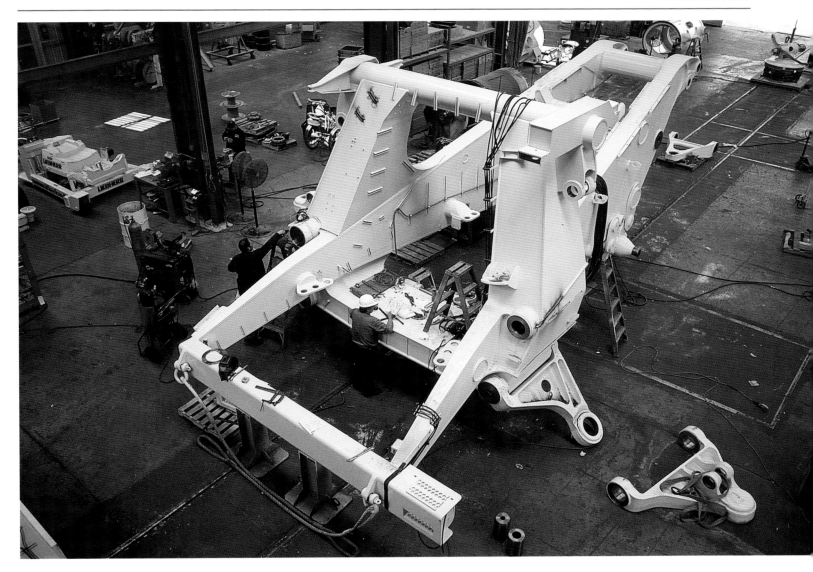

The first Liebherr T-282 hauler frame nears completion at the Baxter Springs, Kansas, plant in August 1998. This frame design, fabricated from high-strength nickel-copper alloy steel and designed for 360-plus-ton payloads, is the strongest ever created by the company. It carries a 60,000-hour warranty, one of the best in the industry.

This prototype T-282 hauler was powered by a Detroit Diesel/MTU 16V4000 diesel, capable of producing 2,750 gross horsepower. The radiator core, as the one used in the Komatsu 320-ton truck, is an L&M Mesabi unit.

The first 930E Komatsu built was shipped to its Illinois proving grounds for performance and component testing in May 1995. This truck serves as the main test bed for all alterations and upgrades the series will receive throughout the model's production run. The second 930E assembled was sent to Fording River Coal in British Columbia, Canada, while the third unit found its first home at ASARCO's Ray Mine in Arizona. It was important early in the development of the 930E that trucks be placed in mining operations that could offer extremes in cold and hot weather situations. Since the AC drive system was a completely new feature on a Haulpak truck, engineers needed to see how it would perform in the brutal winter months of British Columbia, as well as the sweltering heat of the Arizona summer.

As the 930E has matured in the marketplace, Komatsu engineers have kept it on a steady diet of improvements and upgrades. In late 1999, the truck was released as the improved 930E-2 series. This model, often referred to as the Bigfoot truck, has many significant mechanical alterations designed to increase the truck's overall productivity and reliability. Engineers addressed premature tire wear problems in some of the earlier trucks by replacing the original tires with new 50/90R57 radials. These helped measurably, but the real answer was a jump to a larger tire and rim design. The 930E-2 is Komatsu's first hauler to utilize 63-inch rims, instead of the usual 57-inchers. Mounted on these are meaty 53/80R63 radials, some of the largest in the industry for off-highway haulers. Along with the DDC/MTU 16V4000 engine, an optional Cummins QSK60, four-cycle, 16-cylinder powerplant is now offered, rated at 2,700 gross horsepower and 2,550 flywheel horsepower. This engine was thoroughly tested by Komatsu in specially prepared 830E haulers to make sure it could handle service in the 930E-2 series.

Even with all of these upgrades, the 930E-2 still is rated as a 320-ton hauler. When the 930E was introduced, it weighed in at 411,300 pounds empty and 1,034,000

shakedown to test the operation of the on-board computers, the brakes, and all other major systems. Only then is the truck certified as ready for service. From this point, all maintenance, upgrades, and repairs on the truck are handled by the mine owner's trained mechanics. Each mining operation has full on-site repair facilities large enough for a driver to pull a truck the size of the 930E straight in and raise the dump body to maximum height. These maintenance bays are so large and well equipped that entire trucks the size of the 930E can be taken apart, right down to the bare frame and reassembled.

The front view of the first T-282, in September 1998, really puts the mass of the truck into perspective. The T-282's outside tire width of 28 feet, 7 inches guarantees you won't see one of these coming down your street anytime soon. At this stage, the dump body has yet to be installed.

pounds loaded. Today's 930E-2 weighs in empty at 442,214 pounds with the DDC/MTU engine and 446,034 pounds with the Cummins unit. Maximum loaded weight is 1,100,000 pounds, or 550 tons.

At the time of this writing, over 160 of the giant 930Es are at work around the world, with more being built every day. The 930E series of mining trucks was the first shot fired in the battle of the production ultra-haulers, and it seems that Komatsu was right on target with this one.

Liebherr T-282 and TI-272

Liebherr, after building large hydraulic mining excavators for years, entered the mining hauler business in 1995 when it purchased WISEDA, Ltd., of Baxter Springs, Kansas. Through the purchase, it acquired WISEDA's legendary King of the Lode hauler line and formed a new subsidiary company, Liebherr Mining Truck. In January 1996, this name was changed to Liebherr Mining Equipment Company.

Behind the grill of the T-282 rests a 2,750-gross horsepower, 16-cylinder Detroit Diesel/MTU. An optional 2,700-gross horsepower Cummins QSK60 unit is also available. Though these engines are large, there is plenty of extra room in the truck's engine bay to accommodate even larger engines, in the 3,400-horsepower class range when they become available sometime in the near future.

WISEDA was founded in 1980 by William Seldon Davis, formerly of KENDAVIS Industries and Unit Rig fame. Davis wanted to build a more advanced type of mining truck. In 1982, he did just that by introducing the industry's first true production two-axle, 220-ton hauler—the KL-2450 King of the Lode. In 1985, the company released the first production 240-plus-ton capacity KL-2450, three years before the Dresser 830E was introduced. WISEDA was a company with a solid history of engineering accomplishments in producing innovative mining trucks. All it really needed was a little more capital and the diversified manufacturing background of a company like Liebherr to put it on a level playing field with the likes of Komatsu and Caterpillar.

The WISEDA hauler had several key design elements. Massive frame rails, multiple tubular cross-members, and high-strength nickel-copper alloy steel gave the hauler one of the strongest frames in the industry. The front suspension system was unique, in that it provided a dual parallel control arm arrangement that improved handling and extended tire life. The hauler also utilized the Marsh Mellow Spring System, developed by Firestone. Two stacked pads in the front and single pads in the rear absorbed road shock and loading impact, while providing a comfortable ride. The advanced frame and suspension designs allowed WISEDA to offer one of the best frame guarantees in the business. In fact, to date, not one WISEDA/Liebherr hauler frame has ever failed in service.

As mining operations started to favor the Komatsu 930E, Liebherr knew that to compete successfully in the near future, it was going to need its own 300-plus-ton truck. During the early design phase in 1996, the company set a target payload rating of 320 tons. At this point the truck was identified as the KL-2640. Its diesel-electric drivetrain layout would be based around the Siemens AC drive system. The heart of the Siemens AC haul truck system is the twin-inverter system that transforms the DC bus voltage into variable frequency AC current for the wheel motors. This is done with eight air-cooled power modules,

The Liebherr T-282 is a massive mining hauler, capable of hauling 360-plus tons of material, in this case, coal. The prototype truck is fitted with a modified coal body with tailgate for hauling coal on the long, flat haul roads of the Black Thunder Mine in Wright, Wyoming. Height to the top of the spill guard canopy from ground level is 24 feet, 3 inches. Tires are superwide 55/80R63 hauler type radials, mounted on 63-inch diameter wheels. *Liebherr Mining Equipment*

Shown at Terex Mining's Unit Rig assembly plant in Tulsa, Oklahoma, in April 2000, is the prototype MT-5500. Not quite completed yet, it is undergoing engine running tests, including a cooling system check, and the loading of the truck's computer software, which enables the engine and AC drive systems to communicate and function together.

packaged in a rugged enclosure designed for harsh mining duty. Hermetically sealed modules contain an environmentally safe cooling medium to enhance heat transfer to the cooling air. This design is one of the most compact and powerful inverters on the market. Another reason to go with Siemens was that the GE AC drive system for mining haulers was codeveloped with Komatsu and intended only for Komatsu's use for the time being.

During 1997, the big truck program was renamed the KL-2680 and given a new target payload of 340 tons. In 1998, the truck was officially named the T-282. In addition to the new name, the hauler got an increased capacity rating of 360 tons. To make this payload rating viable, the T-282 was designed around 63-inch rims instead of standard 57-inch units. The bigger rims also carried big, meaty Michelin 55/80R63 radial tires. At the time, these were the largest hauler tires in the world. When the T-282 was officially unveiled in October 1998, it carried the title of the world's largest diesel-electric, AC drive haul truck.

The prototype T-282 was manufactured entirely at Liebherr's Baxter Springs plant. The T-282 built on the strengths of the company's other large hauler, the T-262 (KL-2450). Like all other WISEDA/Liebherr haulers, the front suspension system is of a dual control arm arrangement, now with nitrogen/oil struts. The rubber "Marsh Mellow" suspension system, however, disappeared in the early 1990s. Engines specified for the T-282 were the same as those found in the latest Komatsu 930E-2—the DDC/MTU 16V4000 and Cummins QSK60. Power ratings of 2,750 gross horsepower are available from both powerplants. Empty weight of the T-282 is 457,000 pounds, and the truck averages 1,177,000 pounds loaded.

The assembly of the big Liebherr is similar to any other diesel-electric-drive truck. But Liebherr takes it one step further by completely assembling the unit, minus dump body, prior to shipment. This allows for full on-site operational testing of all of the hauler's functions, including dump hoists, brakes, and engine drive system. The Baxter Springs plant has a special test track where the T-282 can be brought up to speed to test full panic braking situations. Once these running tests are completed, the truck chassis is disassembled into shippable component sizes. These tests help assure the customer that when the truck arrives at the mine site, it will be ready for action in mere days.

The prototype T-282 truck was shipped to its first home at Thunder Basin Coal Company's Black Thunder Mine in the Powder River Basin of Wyoming in October 1998. In 1999 it was followed by three more units, one of which was delivered to the Jacobs Ranch mine in the PRB,

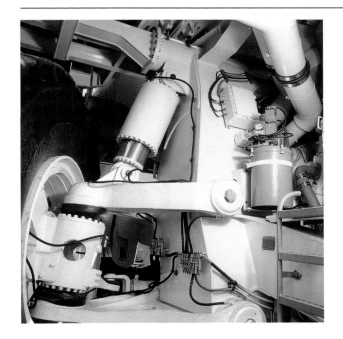

Close-up detail of the front suspension system on a Liebherr mining hauler—in this case, the 320-ton-capacity TI-272—shows how the wheel assembly connects into the parallel control arms. These arms transmit braking, cornering, and steering loads to the main frame. *Liebherr Mining Equipment*

When viewed from the rear, the Liebherr TI-272 looks like no other ultra-hauler in production. The wide-spaced frame rails do not use a center axle housing for rigidity. Instead, the dump body itself is a main structural component of the truck. The wide-spaced wheel mountings, suspended off two independent axle struts, give the hauler superior handling and stability in wet and muddy conditions. *Liebherr Mining Equipment*

and two which make their home with Klemke Mining of Fort McMurray in northern Alberta. These early preproduction trucks have performed so well that the T-282 is now classified as a 360-plus-ton hauler, with the potential to go even higher in the not too distant future.

As impressive as the new T-282 is, Liebherr is currently testing a diesel-electric haul truck, identified as the TI-272, that has serious design innovations not found on any other mining truck in the world. This truck's rear frame and axle-mountings, and its weight-saving designs, are truly on the cutting edge of haul truck technology.

Designed in cooperation with Broken Hill Properties (BHP) of Australia, the prototype "proof of concept" truck was initially referred to as the ILMT (Innovative Large Mining Truck) and then as the IL-2600. In May 1996 the completed truck began testing at the Saraji Coal Mine in Queensland, Australia. The mine is owned by Central Queensland Coal Association and operated by BHP Coal Pty., Ltd. This prototype hauler carried a 240-ton payload.

The rear view of the Unit Rig MT-5500 shows off the truck's massive rear width, which measures 29 feet, 8 inches across. Tires are 55/80R63 radials, mounted on 63-inch diameter rims. Note the design of the General Atomics/PCS retarding forced air grid system mounted on the upper right side of the deck. Its radial design and compact proportions follow from the company's extensive work in rail transit engines and operating systems.

The massive main rear hydraulic service brakes on the MT-5500 are actually used to bring the truck to a complete stop only during low-speed travel, with most of the braking power being supplied by the electric traction motors. The heat generated by the traction motors is dissipated through the dynamic retarding forced-air grid system mounted on the upper deck.

The goal of the joint truck development between Liebherr and BHP was to reduce the total life cycle costs of operation of a rear-dump mining truck by at least 15 percent. Weight of the hauler is reduced by the elimination of the rear axle drive housing. In its place, the dump box acts as an integral part of the frame structure, working in parallel with the frame at all times. This allows the rear tires to be spaced evenly across the back of the truck, with widely spaced suspension struts on individual axle boxes,

The front of the MT-5500 clearly shows the unique design of the truck's staggered stepladder system, which is found on all Unit Rig MT-series haulers, and is an industry exclusive. Its design makes getting on and off the truck, especially in wet and icy conditions, much safer.

The MT-5500 nears completion as its dump body is slowly lowered into place on the chassis. Customarily, the dump box would be shipped directly to the customer's mine site from the subcontractors who build them for Unit Rig. But in this case, the first body was shipped to Tulsa for the official dedication of the truck on April 2, 2000.

not unlike the design of the old VCON 3006 prototype from 1971. The rear wheel motors can be specified with either AC or DC systems, depending on the customer's requirements. In July 1997, after successful testing of the prototype IL-2600, BHP announced a license agreement with Liebherr to begin production of the 300-ton-capacity version of the truck.

The first production TI-272 hauler was built at Liebherr's Newport News, Virginia, facilities. It was shipped in September 1999 to Peabody's Lee Ranch Mine in New Mexico. Originally rated at 300 tons, the truck had its payload rating raised to 320 tons. The truck was equipped with Siemens AC drive wheel motors and a DDC/MTU 16V4000 diesel engine rated at 2,700 gross horsepower. A Cummins QSK60 rated at 2,500 gross horsepower is also available. The TI-272 rides on special Bridgestone 46/90R57VELSB low-profile/low-pressure radial tires. Slightly smaller 44/80R57 tires can also be specified to meet a customer's particular needs. After completing its initial shakedown testing phase, the first TI-272 was officially handed over to Lee Ranch mining officials on January 4, 2000, as fit and ready for duty. A few months later, this same truck was moved up to the PRB to Triton's North Rochelle coal mine in May 2000.

Liebherr has positioned itself well in the new millennium, with haulers such as the T-282 and TI-272. Both trucks are completely new designs, using the latest and most innovative manufacturing technologies available to mining equipment producers. Both models have plenty of room to grow to meet future customers' mining needs. For instance, the T-282 has some 2 feet of extra space behind the front radiator grille and bumper area, which could easily accommodate one of the more powerful engines currently being developed by the engine manufacturers.

Unit Rig MT-5500

It was only a matter of time before the company that practically invented the modern diesel-electric-drive mining hauler would finally introduce an ultra-hauler of its

very own. Unit Rig, which is a key part of Terex Mining of Tulsa, Oklahoma, unveiled its heavy hitter, the MT-5500, at its Tulsa assembly plant on April 2, 2000.

The MT-5500 is rated as a 360-ton-capacity hauler. It was designed around an AC drive system provided by Power Conversion Systems (PCS), which is a division of General Atomics, headquartered in San Diego, California. The company was founded in 1955 as a division of General Dynamics, with the purpose of exploring the peaceful uses of atomic energy. Today, General Atomics is privately owned and is one of the world's leading resources for high technology systems development. Its PCS division builds AC power systems for rail and transit uses. This is the first time a PCS-designed AC drive system has been used in a mining hauler.

Development on Unit Rig's big boy got under way in 1997, when it was referred to as the MT-4800. In mid-

The MT-5500 uses a drop-center fabricated box-section beam front axle, which is simple in design, but extremely strong. It is used on all MT-series mining trucks built by Unit Rig, though not on the scale found on the MT-5500.

1998, Unit Rig finally settled on the MT-5500 identification. Though originally planned as a 340-ton hauler, it was uprated to 360 tons upon its official introduction. The MT-5500 shares a few of its key equipment choices with its rivals. It is designed around the use of 63-inch rims with 55/80R63 radial tires. The diesel-electric drive system is

Shown at Caterpillar's Decatur, Illinois, assembly plant on September 29, 1998, the first pilot 797 makes its way down the shop floor. The design of the 797's front suspension system is unique to the Caterpillar truck. It uses a single self-contained, oil-pneumatic suspension cylinder per wheel, bolted to the upper and lower cast frame members for maximum support. The braking system on the big Cat truck is a sealed four-wheel, forced oil-cooled multiple disc arrangement.

powered by the tried and tested DDC/MTU 16V4000 engine, rated at 2,800 gross horsepower. The new Cummins QSK60 is also available, with an output of 2,700 gross horsepower.

Several features of the MT-5500 are not shared with any other ultra-hauler. These include its massive front axle beam design, which is extremely strong, durable, and simple. Another unique feature is a rear axle housing mounted to a frame cross-member by a large diameter nose-cone bearing patented by Unit Rig, eliminating fatigue-prone brackets. Further, the innovative General Atomics radial designed forced air grid system is more compact and efficient than competing designs. The frame of the hauler is of a welded deep double box-section design, with steel castings used only for the cylinder mounts for the dump body. All in all, the MT-5500 is one serious mining hauler.

Unit Rig has many of the larger fabrications for its haulers subcontracted out to specialized manufacturers with the latest machine tool technology. All completed subassemblies are shipped to the Tulsa plant for final quality control inspection and assembly. From there, the trucks are shipped out to mining operations around the world. The dump body and tires are shipped directly from their point of origin to meet up with the rest of the truck at the customer's mine site. In the case of the prototype MT-5500, the dump box and tires were shipped to the Tulsa plant for final fitting and full testing on the first unit.

The MT-5500 is certainly a big truck, in keeping with the overall design look established by the company's popular 260-ton-capacity MT-4400. The MT-5500's rounded radiator housing and wraparound windshield give the Unit Rig truck a style all its own. In June 2000, the prototype MT-5500 was shipped to the Jacobs Ranch Coal Mine, south of Gillette, Wyoming, in the Powder River Basin, to start its long-term field testing program. At the time of this writing, another six trucks were awaiting final assembly, destined for mining operations around the globe.

Here is something the Caterpillar 797 can lay sole claim to in the ultra-hauler mining truck category—the only mechanically driven rear differential in the industry. The seven-speed, planetary powershift transmission of the 797 bolts directly to the front of the differential housing.

Caterpillar 797

All of the manufacturers of ultra-hauler trucks believe that the diesel-electric-drive layout is the best possible solution for the mining industry. That is, all except one—Caterpillar.

Caterpillar has been building mechanical drive off-highway trucks since it first unveiled its legendary Model 769 in late 1962. Except for a brief exploration of diesel-electric-drive prototypes during the 1960s, involving the 779, 783, and 786 programs, all of the company's production quarry and mining trucks have been of a mechanical drive layout. The Caterpillar system uses a diesel engine, powershift transmission, driveshafts, and a rear differential. No electric traction motors are used in this type of design.

Caterpillar rocked the mining industry in 1991 when it introduced its first 240-ton-capacity 793 hauler. No one thought that a mechanical drive system could be built that would be able to handle the payload capacities of this hauler class. No one, of course, but Caterpillar. The 793, along with its updated 793B and 793C variations, is now the best-selling 240-ton class hauler in the world, knocking the former champion, the diesel-electric-drive Komatsu 830E, from top position. But could the company compete in the ultra-hauler class, with a mechanical

In 1999, Syncrude Canada, Ltd., started receiving shipments of the new Caterpillar 797 hauler for use at its North Mine, with further trucks arriving in 2000 for the new Aurora Mine. Truck number 101 is the second unit commissioned at the North mining site by Syncrude. Though rated with a nominal payload capacity of 360 tons, the Canadian trucks are often carrying loads in the 380-ton range. Width of the 797 is 30 feet, and its height to the top of the spill guard is 23 feet, 8 inches. *Syncrude Canada*

drivetrain-based truck that the industry basically said couldn't be built? The answer was a resounding yes.

On September 29, 1998, at its Decatur, Illinois, assembly plant, Caterpillar unveiled a truly astounding piece of engineering work—the massive 797. The 797 is simply a huge hauler, designed to carry a payload of 360-plus tons of material. It took Caterpillar only 18 months to make the 797 a reality, from concept to finished prototype. The entire truck was designed with 3D computer technology, using advanced finite element and solid modeling software technology. The 797 uses seven onboard computers to control and monitor all of its vital functions. Caterpillar's other mining haulers shared many design and component aspects, but the 797 is all new, and shares none of its major systems with its little brothers in the product line.

The 797 is powered by a newly developed Cat 3524B EUI (Electronic Unit Injection) aftercooled diesel engine, with four single-stage turbochargers. Power ratings are a whopping 3,400 gross horsepower and 3,211 flywheel horsepower, at just 1,750 rpm. The design is based on two modified 3512 engines, connected in line by an innovative flexible coupling. This is mated to a highly automated, electronically controlled, seven-speed automatic-shift transmission, driving a large rear-mounted modular differential. This is the most sophisticated mechanical drivetrain the company has ever produced.

The load-bearing frame design of the 797 differs from that of the 793C hauler in that it is made up entirely of mild steel castings. Nine major castings are machined for a precise fit before being joined by robotic welders. The company's smaller 793C uses a mixture of box section steel structures, with steel castings in critical areas. The 797 frame design uses far fewer welds and creates a structure that is incredibly strong, suitable for supporting the kinds of loads the truck will face on a daily basis.

Another key factor in the design of the 797 is its use of 63-inch rims. Previously, the largest rims available were 57 inches, the industry standard for haulers with capacities of more than 200 tons. Caterpillar worked closely with Michelin on the development of the tires that would support the massive truck. The tires, new 58/80R63 radials, are simply the state of the art as far as haul trucks are concerned. They have to be if they are going on a truck that is capable of a 40-mile-per-hour top speed, with a full 360-ton plus load on board.

All of those extra mechanical components do add a bit more weight to the truck, compared to its competitors. But with 3,224 flywheel horsepower available, it has little trouble negotiating even the steepest haul roads fully loaded. The 797 is far and away the most powerful ultra-hauler. It is even more powerful than the former heavyweight champ, the Terex 33-19 Titan, which had to make do with only 3,000 flywheel horsepower. The 797 weighs in at approximately 560,000 pounds empty. Compare this to its closest rivals, the Liebherr T-282 at 457,000 pounds, the Terex/Unit Rig MT-5500 at 445,000 pounds, the Komatsu 930E-2 at 442,214 pounds, and the Liebherr TI-272 at 305,000 pounds.

By November 1998, the first 797 had arrived at Cat's Arizona Proving Grounds to start closely monitored field testing and evaluation. In December, it was joined by the second preproduction unit. Starting in June 1999, additional 797 haulers started appearing at large North American mining operations. Full North American release was in 2000, with full worldwide availability in 2001. At the time of this writing, 797 haulers were successfully operating in large open pit mining operations in Arizona, Utah, Wyoming, and northern Alberta, Canada.

When the 797 was first announced, it had a rated payload capacity of 360 tons. At the time of this writing, its capacity is given as 360-plus tons. In the field, the 797 has had little problem handling loads in excess of 360 tons. In Wyoming, working in the Powder River Basin, 797 haulers equipped with massive WOTCO coal bodies are regularly weighing in with loads in the 366- to 386-ton range. Trucks working in the Oil Sands regions of northern Alberta are carrying even more. But the tires are clearly showing the strain. This is probably the one area that is holding back the big Cat truck. In time, this will be solved, and then we will really get to see what this incredible hauling marvel can do. Next stop, 400 tons.

REVOLUTIONARY TEXAS IRON
LETOURNEAU'S GIANT WHEEL LOADERS

Although its name sounds French, LeTourneau is as American as apple pie. Not so long ago, during the 1930s and 1940s, the name of LeTourneau was just as well known in the earthmoving industry as Caterpillar. In fact, the history of LeTourneau is the history of modern earthmoving itself.

Back in 1922, in Stockton, California, a man by the name of Robert Gilmour LeTourneau, with the help of his brother-in-law Ray Peterson, built his first earthmoving scraper out of bits and pieces of metal and electric motors. His second scraper, built a few months later and nicknamed the Gondola, was fabricated by brazing and welding, an industry first for this type of machine. Early 1923 saw his third unit, the much larger Mountain Mover. The fourth built was the Self-Propelled Scraper from late 1923. This unit, with its electric wheel drive, was the first self-propelled scraper ever built. This pattern of building new and improved earthmoving equipment continued for the rest of R. G. LeTourneau's life. He con-

ceived innovation after innovation in the design and production not only of earthmoving machines, but also logging and military equipment, welding technology, and off-shore oil drilling platforms. Like the machines he loved to build, LeTourneau's name appears large on the pages of earthmover history.

The creations of R. G. LeTourneau often pushed the technological boundaries of the time. He would rarely sit back and wait for another supplier to build something he needed to make his creations a reality. When the tire manufacturers refused to build tires of a suitable size for his inventions, he started to design and build his own tire molds and subcontract the molding process to various tire manufacturers in the 1950s and 1960s. LeTourneau is credited as the first manufacturer to put pneumatic tires on a tractor-pulled scraper (in 1932) and the first to design and build a fully self-propelled, rubber-tired scraper, known as the Model A Tournapull (in 1938).

The first L-1800 loader delivered into service works at the Eagle Butte Mine, just north of Gillette, Wyoming. Shipped in July 1994, it was equipped with a 45-cubic-yard combo-bucket, replacing the original 33-cubic-yard rock unit.

At LeTourneau's own steel mill, a ladle filled with refined molten metal, bottom-pours ingots for quality enhancement. After solidification, the ingots are stripped from the molds, and those scheduled for plate products are placed into a soaking pit and heated to the proper temperature for rolling. *LeTourneau*

But of all of R. G. LeTourneau's early inventions, his creation of the earthmoving industry's first internal electric wheel motor ranks as one of his most daring and successful, and expensive, undertakings. His first creation to use this new concept in locomotion was the Tournatow from 1950. Built for the U.S. Air Force, it was the first in a long line of diesel-electric-drive machines to bear the LeTourneau name. In this drivetrain layout, the mechanical connections between the primary power source and the drive wheels, the transmission, driveshafts, and differentials were all replaced by electric generators and wheel motors, powered by a conventional diesel engine. Even today, this is still the key feature found in the company's machines. It is really what a "LeTourneau" is all about.

R. G. LeTourneau, Inc., was officially formed in 1929. Originally headquartered in Stockton, California, it moved its corporate offices in 1935 to Peoria, Illinois, which was also home to the Caterpillar Tractor Company. During the next several years, LeTourneau expanded to include key manufacturing plants in Toccoa, Georgia, in 1939; Rydalmere, Australia, in 1941; Vicksburg, Mississippi, in 1942; and Longview, Texas, in 1946. In 1953, LeTourneau sold the earthmoving equipment division of his company to Westinghouse Air Brake Company, forming the subsidiary firm, LeTourneau-Westinghouse Company R. G. retained ownership of the Longview and Vicksburg facilities, while the others became the property of LeTourneau-Westinghouse. The Longview plant and offices became the new world headquarters for R. G. LeTourneau, Inc. His deal with Westinghouse included a noncompete agreement barring R. G. from building and selling earthmoving equipment commercially for five years. Not included in this deal, however, were logging machinery concepts started before the sale. Also excluded were specialized military earthmoving electric-drive prototypes, since these were seen as military applications only, with no commercial sales potential. In 1955 the company entered the off-shore oil rig drilling platform market with the world's first mobile, self-elevating ocean platform. By

Cutting steel plate to specific sizes is accomplished by gas-oxygen or plasma torching. These systems cut through plating from 3/4-inch to 8-inch thickness like butter. *LeTourneau*

The basic frame structure of the LeTourneau L-1800 is the same as that used in the L-1400 model. The diesel-electric drive system makes assembly much easier because it doesn't require a mechanical drivetrain's transmission, torque converter, and driveshafts.

1958, LeTourneau was allowed to reenter the earthmoving market with the production of an entirely new line of diesel-electric-drive scrapers referred to as Electric-Diggers. These would eventually be sold under the Pacemaker trade name.

During the 1960s, the company produced various types of experimental machines at both plants, some successful and others less so. When it came to the size of his creations, R. G. took a back seat to nobody. And for power—if one or two big Detroit Diesels weren't enough, he'd try adding three, four, or more to the machinery design. LeTourneau's philosophy was quite clear as far as power was concerned. If strapping on an engine in an odd location would help performance, then so be it. Aesthetics was not something he was terribly concerned about. His

creations were pure modular functionality that sometimes looked as if they had leaped off the pages of a science fiction magazine.

After the death of R. G. LeTourneau in June 1969, the company was purchased in 1970 by Marathon Manufacturing Company of Houston, Texas, forming Marathon LeTourneau. By 1979, it became a wholly owned subsidiary of the Penn Central Corporation. Then finally in 1994, the Marathon LeTourneau Company, which by that time was now a subsidiary of the General Cable Corporation, was purchased by Rowan Companies, Inc., of Houston, Texas. Rowan, a major provider of international and domestic offshore contract and drilling services, had purchased many of LeTourneau's oil and gas drilling platforms. One of the first things Rowan put into effect was changing the company's name to LeTourneau, Inc. Eliminating the Marathon part of the name seemed to put everything to right again.

LeTourneau, Inc., world headquarters is still in Longview, where all of the diesel-electric-drive machines are produced. The Vicksburg plant facilities mainly revolve around the fabrication of the massive offshore drilling platforms. The company's key products today include drilling platforms, log stackers, jib cranes, steel, and of course giant mining wheel loaders.

LeTourneau first started building large diesel-electric-drive loaders in 1960 with the rather odd-looking SL-10. This concept was followed by the SL-20, SL-30, and SL-40, all in 1964. In 1965, an SL-15 prototype was built. All of these used a rack-and-pinion type of design, driven by electric motors to work the loading and dumping functions. R. G. had a firm belief that hydraulic systems were too inefficient and complicated. But finally, LeTourneau engineers prevailed and in 1968 a prototype loader, initially referred to as the XL-1 Letric-Loader, was built, using full hydraulic cylinder controls. This prototype went on to become the L-700. Other models to follow included the L-500 in 1969, the L-800 in 1975, the L-600 in 1976, and the large L-1200 in 1978.

As the L-1800 progresses through the assembly process, it is fitted with factory "yard" tires and loading bucket. These are not the components that will ship with the final machine and are just used around the factory grounds during the loader's final predelivery testing. At the rear can be seen the Power Resistor (dynamic braking) Grids, swung open in the radiator area, which dissipate the kinetic energy of the loader's electric drive system during braking.

On a parallel assembly line, an L-1100 nears its final stages of the build process. Soon it will have its wheel motors installed, along with yard test tires and bucket, for a brief proving ground workout.

Workers make final adjustments just before preliminary engine start-up, just to make sure all is as it should be. The gray primed box on the upper-right is the KLENZ air filtration system. This self-cleaning unit filters the air for both the engine and traction motor cooling system. It purges dirt and dust from the filter elements with a blast of air every 60 seconds to maintain filter-cleaning efficiency.

Today, the company builds five sizes of wheel loaders, from big to simply enormous. These are the L-1000, introduced in 1982; the L-1100 from 1986; the L-1350 from 1999; the L-1400 from 1990; and top-of-the-line L-1800 from 1993. At the time of this writing, the L-1800 is not only the world's largest diesel-electric-drive wheel loader, it is the largest built of any kind. There are other big mining loaders on the market, but none within striking distance of the L-1800's hefty 100,000-pound bucket load capacity, averaging 33 cubic yards per bite.

All of the loaders are built entirely at the Longview, Texas, plant. This plant, which was established in 1946, is unique among the world's manufacturing facilities. Most notable are five, semispherical, demountable aluminum building structures that house various fabrication and welding production areas. The first of these buildings dates back to mid-1953, when evangelist Dr. Billy Graham, a long-time friend of R. G. LeTourneau, asked him to design and build a structure capable of being assembled and disassembled for transport around England for a series of evangelical crusades. LeTourneau designed the aluminum structure with a 300-foot diameter and a height of 85 feet, capable of holding 12,000 people. The prototype building, built at Longview, was to be tested at a Billy Graham crusade in Michigan. State building inspectors, however, refused to allow the structure to be erected there because it did not meet the state's building codes. After this setback, the English government indicated that it too would deny permission to use the building, citing economic reasons. So the building remained exactly were it was first erected, in front of the main plant area in Texas. But the structure did provide an excellent, cost-effective means of expanding manufacturing operations. So much so, that four more of the structures have been added over the years.

Along with the five semispherical structures, there is the main plant, where all of the loaders are actually built in an assembly line process. Behind the plant is LeTourneau's very own steel mill. This mill, which went on line in 1951, produces various grades of steel for the products built by the company. The mill also serves customers on the outside, including several major steel distributors and service centers, fabricators, and manufacturers throughout the world. Steel produced in the mill is used in building the loaders' frame assemblies, as well as the main lift arms and all structural components. These components are the most critical and heavy fabrications in the building process. Since the LeTourneau mill specializes in steel plating in thicknesses from 3/4 inch to 8 inches, thinner steel grades are purchased from outside venders. This steel is used in such areas as the cab and rear deck areas.

All of the company's loaders use the latest computer-aided design (CAD) and computer-aided manufacturing (CAM) techniques, including finite stress analysis in key high-stress areas of the loader. The absence of major mechanical components, such as transmissions and driveshafts, due to the use of electric drive, simplifies the building process of the big loaders. LeTourneau designs and builds all of the major components for its electrical drive systems. For 50 years, the company has made all of its own electric wheel motors. Other manufacturers, such as those building haulers, buy all of their motors from outside suppliers, such as General Electric and Siemens, both of which make state-of-the-art products. But the LeTourneau DC motors built for wheel loader use are custom made to meet the heavy-duty demands put upon them by the working cycles of such machines. Along with the wheel motors, the company builds its own line of generators to supply current to these motors. The generator is mounted directly to the diesel engine in the loader,

The finished machine is always shipped to the new customer's mine site with a complete set of loader tires. Additional tires will come direct from the tire manufacturer of the owner's choosing. The tires shown are size 53.5/85-57,76PR(L-5), which are more than 12 feet in diameter. These tires are meant for use with the L-1800.

from which it gets its power. All of the electronic controls for these systems use solid-state circuit boards made on the premises.

Another design feature of LeTourneau's loaders is the use of carburized, machined ball-and-socket joints in all pivoting, load-bearing points. The spherical shape of the ball-and-socket provides a large load-bearing surface to handle the stress and torsion flexing of the machine from any direction. The loader's two main frame sections are

After successful preliminary testing, an L-1800 is partially dismantled for its final paint process, after which the loader will be shipped out in component pieces to fit either truck or rail transport, depending on its ultimate destination.

connected by an upper and lower ball-and-socket joint, which enables the machine to articulate to the left and right. Without a mechanical driveshaft running through this area, the LeTourneau loaders can achieve a very tight turning radius. Another benefit of eliminating the mechanical drivetrain is a lower center of gravity, helping to maintain the loader's balance during loading cycles.

All of the company's loaders are custom built to order. Depending on geographic locations and mine requirements, the loaders can be specified with various diesel engine and tire options. Even the buckets are specified for the exact material the loader will be working in. The machines are also set up to meet any special environmental restrictions, such as those governing exhaust systems and noise suppression. And yes, an am/fm stereo CD-cassette system is also available for those long days and nights at the controls.

Once the loader is fully assembled, it receives a set of "yard" tires and rims, along with a test loading bucket. Then it is put through a series of performance tests to make sure all engine and hydraulic functions are up to performance specifications. Any problems are found early on and are corrected before the loader is dismantled and shipped off the premises. After all testing is completed, the loader is cleaned thoroughly, partially dismantled into shipping subassemblies and painted. Because LeTourneau's machines go all over the globe, they are shipped accordingly, by truck, rail, or ship, and sometimes by all three methods. These giant loaders can be found working in North America, South America, Europe, Australia, South Africa, and Russia.

The largest wheel loader in the world at the time of this writing is the mighty L-1800. LeTourneau officially announced this machine in December 1993, with the first machine delivered to a customer in 1994. The L-1800's greatest asset, besides its large bucket, is its mobility. The loader can work in various areas in a mine during any given shift because of its ability to relocate itself quickly. This is something that is just not practical for a large cable shovel or hydraulic front-shovel. When any of a mine's

Once at a mine site, a LeTourneau loader, in this case an L-1400, goes together in a matter of days. LeTourneau personnel from the local distributor assemble the loader to make sure all critical systems function properly. *LeTourneau*

As the L-1400 is assembled on-site, larger structures, such as the main boom, are lifted into place by heavy-lift cranes already at the mine site. The service dealer's truck boom crane is only meant to handle smaller components. *LeTourneau*

main shovels are shut down for maintenance or a break-down, the L-1800 can be brought in immediately from another work assignment to continue loading haulers. This way, the trucks do not have to be reassigned or sit idle during shovel repairs. The L-1800 has the ability to load 240-ton-capacity haulers, as well as 320-plus-ton-capacity trucks, with its high-lift boom option. A loader the size of the L-1800 wears many hats in today's modern mining operations. Its versatility makes it the jack-of-all-trades in the world mining industry.

As mentioned, the customer has the choice between two engine options for the L-1800. During the first few years of production, the Cummins K-1800E, four-cycle, turbocharged and aftercooled diesel, or the Detroit Diesel 16V149TI DDEC III, two-cycle, turbocharged and inter-cooled engine could be selected. Both powerplants were 16-cylinder engines, rated at 1,800 flywheel horsepower, with optional 2,000-flywheel horsepower versions of both diesels available. Today's L-1800 has the choice of either a Cummins QSK 60 diesel, or a Detroit Diesel/MTU D4000 16V DDEC. Both engines are four-cycle, turbocharged and aftercooled, 16-cylinder diesels, rated at 2,000 flywheel horsepower each. These engines power a single LeTourneau 12B AC generator, which supplies current to four LeTourneau J-2 DC traction wheel motors, giving the loader full-time four-wheel drive. Since the loader has no transmission, the speed range is infinitely variable between 0 and 11 miles per hour, both forward and reverse.

The L-1800 rides on massive 53.5/85-57,76PR(L-5) tires, mounted on 44-57 rims. Wider 55/80R-57(L-5) radials are also available. Average life of a tire is around 5,000 hours of running time. Tires of this size range between $30,000 and $50,000 each! So care of the tires, such as maintaining proper inflation pressures, is essential for a long working life. A major sidewall cut is almost certain death for the tire and a major hit to the owner's bottom line.

Overall working weight of the L-1800 is around 480,000 pounds with standard lift arms, and 485,000 with the high-lift option. Bucket size is 33 cubic yards for the

This later model L-1800 working at the Barrick Goldstrike Mine, near Elko, Nevada, in October 1998, is equipped with the first generation of the Klenz air filtration system. It is also matched with the standard 33-cubic-yard rock bucket.

standard version and 31 for the high-lift. Total operating payload is 100,000 pounds and 94,000 pounds, respectively. An optional 55-cubic-yard coal loading bucket is also offered for the L-1800. This coal loading bucket is the largest currently offered for a wheel loader. The first of these special buckets was installed on an L-1800 in 1998, on a machine working at the North Antelope Rochelle Complex Coal Mine in Wyoming's Powder River Basin.

The L-1800's little brother in the LeTourneau loader lineup is the L-1400. In fact, the two machines are very much alike, except in the propulsion system and bucket sizes. The L-1400 uses slightly smaller LeTourneau M-40 DC traction motors, though the generator is unchanged. Engines are the same specified in the L-1800, except they are set at 1,800 flywheel horsepower output. Standard tires are 50/80-57, 68PR(L-4) on 36-57 rims, but larger optional

THE MECHANICAL-DRIVE ALTERNATIVES

LeTourneau is the world's only manufacturer of large diesel-electric drive wheel loaders, while Caterpillar and Komatsu, the industry's number one and two ranked heavy-equipment manufacturers, produce mechanical drive-train layout wheel loaders. Caterpillar's entry in the large wheel loader arena is the 994 series, the best-selling ultra-large mining wheel loader of all time. The Komatsu machine, the new WA1200-3, is the company's first try at building this size of loading tool from the ground up.

Caterpillar's 994 wheel loader was first introduced in late 1990 and is classified as a 23-cubic yard machine. It has a 70,000-pound payload limit and was the largest loader ever built by the company at that time. The loader was completely designed around a mechanical drive layout. The Caterpillar 3516 EUI diesel engine, rated at 1,336 gross horsepower and 1,250 flywheel horsepower, supplied the power. The transmission was a Cat-designed planetary, three-speed powershift unit. Overall working weight of the big Cat was a healthy 390,300 pounds.

The prototype Cat 994 was built at the company's Decatur, Illinois, plant, but production machines are built at the Joliet, Illinois, facilities.

The first Caterpillar 994 loaders were originally equipped with 49.5-57 68 L-4 series tires that were just barely adequate for a wheel loader of this size. But at the time, it was the only choice available from the tire manufacturers. Soon, the tire manufacturers released a larger design, the 53.5/85-57, built only for wheel loader use. The tire made an immediate difference in the performance and productivity of the loader. Even larger 55/80 R57 radial tires were introduced as options, giving customers a much wider choice and giving them the ability to match tire-type to particular working conditions.

The 994 when equipped with its standard 23-cubic yard bucket could load 150-ton haulers in four passes, 195-ton units in five to six passes, and 240-ton trucks with seven passes, when equipped with the high-lift loader arm arrangement. However, it cannot load haulers in the 360-ton capacity class, such as the company's giant 797.

In December 1998, Caterpillar introduced an upgrade of the 994 in the form of the 994D. From the outside, little was changed, but internally, there were significant changes. The new model was now equipped with the improved 3516B EUI diesel, now rated at 1,375 gross horsepower, with flywheel output remaining the same as the 994. The revamped steering controls

Caterpillar must be doing something right with its 994 loader series. Rated at 23 cubic yards, it is not the largest-capacity machine on the market, but it is the best-selling large mining loader by far, with over 200 units in service worldwide. *Caterpillar*

The Komatsu WA1200-3 meets the company's needs for a large mining wheel loader. However, those needs were formerly served by the short-lived KDC 4000 "Haulpak" machine. This completely new design shares nothing with the discontinued 4000 loader. The first prototype WA1200-3 loaders was tested in 1998 and availability was officially announced in 1999. The first North American units began arriving on American shores by mid-2000. *KMS*

were a welcome new addition for the operator. The steering wheel was replaced by a joystick control mounted to the left of the operator's seat, called the Cat Steering and Transmission Integrated Control system (STIC). Caterpillar offers the STIC control system, along with other technical upgrade packages, that can be retrofitted to existing pre-D series units. Operating weight of the current 994D model is 421,600 pounds.

Komatsu officially introduced its big Mountain Mover WA1200-3 wheel loader at the International Mining Exposition (AIMEX) held in Sydney, Australia, in October 1999. Like the Caterpillar 994D, the WA1200-3 is a mechanical drivetrain layout. But the big Komatsu carries just a slightly larger bucket, which is rated at 26.2 cubic yards.

The WA1200-3 is powered by the state-of-the-art, 16-cylinder Cummins Quantum QSK60 diesel engine, rated at 1,715 gross horsepower and 1,560 flywheel horsepower. Transmission is a full powershift, three-speed unit, equipped with Komatsu's Electronic Control Modulation Valve (ECMV), which automatically selects the optimum gear to match the unit to its working conditions,

such as travel speed and engine speed. Other performance features include operator adjustable traction control and Komatsu Tire Saver, which senses wheel slippage electronically and reduces it automatically. Articulated steering, transmission, and shift controls are joystick mounted for easy operator manipulation.

The WA1200-3 comes standard with big 55.5/80-57,68PR tires, with optional ultra-wide base 65/65-57,62PR units developed especially for this loader. These optional wide base tires are currently the largest production tires offered for a wheel loader of any make. Full operating weight of the WA1200-3 with the standard tires is 452,390 pounds and 463,400 with the optional wide base type. When the high-lift boom is specified, weights are 459,200 pounds and 470,200 respectively. The high-lift boom carries a slightly smaller 23.5-cubic yard bucket.

Even though Komatsu builds its WA800-3 and WA900-3 mining loaders at its Peoria, Illinois, assembly plant, the WA1200-3 is built entirely in Japan. The prototype WA1200-3 machines first saw mining action in Australia in 1998, with the first North American units arriving in May 2000.

LeTourneau fabricates all of its own buckets at the Longview, Texas, plant. Any type and size can be built to meet a customer's exact working conditions. LeTourneau can also equip the buckets with its own TLC (Total Lip Coverage) Bucket System, which uses high-strength structural alloy steel instead of castings, for the tooth points and adapters. These provide superior protection for the lip of the bucket, along with increasing the effectiveness and production rate of the unit while digging. *LeTourneau*

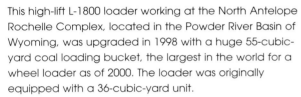

This high-lift L-1800 loader working at the North Antelope Rochelle Complex, located in the Powder River Basin of Wyoming, was upgraded in 1998 with a huge 55-cubic-yard coal loading bucket, the largest in the world for a wheel loader as of 2000. The loader was originally equipped with a 36-cubic-yard unit.

Unveiled in 1999, the L-1350 introduces all new state-of-the-art features into LeTourneau's family of diesel-electric-drive loaders. Rated as a 26-cubic-yard machine, it features full digital controls and monitoring systems, as well as joy-stick hand controls for the operator.

combinations are also available, like those found on the L-1800. The L-1400 is rated at 28 cubic yards, with an 84,000-pound operating payload. With the high-lift setup, the figures are 26 cubic yards and 78,000 pounds. Operating weight of the two loader variations is 445,000 pounds and 450,000 respectively.

The newest addition to the LeTourneau loader line is the L-1350, which was introduced in 1999. The L-1350 is the company's first diesel-electric-drive loader to be equipped with microprocessor-based full digital control and monitoring systems, with driver joy-stick controls replacing the conventional steering wheel. This state-of-the-art loader is rated as a 26-cubic-yard machine, capable

of handling 80,000-pound loads. Weighing in at 390,000 pounds, it is just a bit smaller than the L-1400. It is likely that once the L-1350 is fully established in the marketplace, the L-1400 will be phased out. But at the time of this writing, both are offered to the mining industry.

The tradition of building larger-than-life earthmoving equipment bearing the legendary LeTourneau name is alive and well in Texas. The name might not be as recognizable to the average person as it was decades ago, but to mining operators and owners, LeTourneau means productivity. If R. G. LeTourneau could see the L-1800 loader of today, no doubt he would be proud to have his name displayed on it—though he might scratch his head in disbelief at all of those hydraulic cylinders and hoses.

FLUID POWER
THE O&K RH400 HYDRAULIC EXCAVATOR

In the early 1950s, the introduction of the industry's first fully hydraulic, crawler-mounted excavator would signal the beginning of the end of the small to midsize contractor type of cable shovels and backhoe machines. The first of these new hydraulic excavators to reach full production was the German-built Demag (Deutsche Maschinenfabrik AG) B-504 in 1954. This was a small machine, to be sure, but it wouldn't be long before manufacturers would offer larger and more powerful models to the mining industry.

The French firm of Poclain is credited with introducing the first large, fully hydraulic mining excavator, in the form of the 151-ton EC1000, in 1971. As big as the EC1000 was, it would be eclipsed by an even larger machine by the end of the decade. That hydraulic excavator was the groundbreaking O&K RH300. The RH300, built by Orenstein & Koppel of Dortmund, Germany, and introduced to the earthmoving industry in 1979, was the first machine of its type to break the 500-ton operating

weight barrier. Designed as a hydraulic front shovel, it weighed in at a then-staggering 549 tons, equipped with a 29-cubic-yard bucket. Its power output of 2,320 flywheel horsepower was substantial at the time.

Orenstein & Koppel, whose company history dates back to 1876, was founded in Berlin by Benno Orenstein and Arthur Koppel. The firm spent its early years building portable and narrow-gauge rail equipment that could be moved quickly, including small side-dump tippers. At the turn of the century, the company began building bucket chain excavators at its Spandau works. Made up of wood and iron components, they were powered by steam or paraffin. In 1904, O&K built its first bucket chain excavator fabricated entirely out of iron. This was followed in 1908 with the development of the company's first shovel excavator on rails, at its Spandau works. In 1911, Benno Orenstein purchased a 93 percent holding in Lubecker-Maschinenbau Gesellschaft (LMG), a longtime German manufacturer of floating dredgers (since 1876) and steam

In 1997, the O&K RH400 officially took over the top spot in the mining industry as the world's largest hydraulic excavator. The first unit, pictured, weighed in at 910 tons. More advanced and improved versions weigh 965 tons dry, with a working weight of just over 980 tons.

The O&K RH300 hydraulic front shovel was the first such machine to break the 500-ton operating weight barrier. Shown at the Dortmund factory in October 1979, it is painted in the colors of Northern Strip Mining Ltd. (NSM) of the United Kingdom. It would go to work at NSM's Donnington Extension Coal Mine in January 1980. The RH300's poor reception in the marketplace has less to do with the machine's performance than with the worldwide economic recession of the early 1980s, which wiped out almost all prospective buyers for a machine of this size.
Terex Mining

bucket chain excavators (since 1882). This company would finally be fully integrated into O&K in 1950, but only after two world wars and the eventual rebuilding of Germany itself.

In 1961, O&K introduced its first full production hydraulic excavator, the RH5. This small hydraulic excavator, whose first full year of production was 1962, would set the stage for a whole new range of machines, establishing O&K as one of the leading manufacturers of hydraulic machines in Europe and beyond. O&K started offering the mining industry larger hydraulic machines in 1971 with its 124-ton RH60, and in late 1975 with the 150-ton RH75. Finally, in 1979, the release of the RH300 would firmly cement the company's reputation as a builder of world-class, ultralarge mining excavators.

O&K would build only two more RH300 front shovels during the 1980s, mainly due to the worldwide economic recession that was strangling new product sales. The second RH300 was shown at the 1980 Bauma equipment trade fair in Germany, but was shipped back to the Dortmund plant after the exposition for further testing. It would never be sold. The third machine, the only electric-powered unit, was destined for Codelco's Chuquicamata Copper Mine in Chile in 1987. Parts from the dismantled second machine kept the first and third machines supplied with cost-effective spares.

In 1986 the 600-ton H485 front shovel of the German firm Mannesmann Demag would take the crown of the world's largest hydraulic excavator away from the RH300. The heaviest of the three O&K machines built was the third unit, the RH300E, which tipped the scales at 566 tons. Just more than 10 years passed before O&K regained top billing from Demag. The machine to do it was O&K's incredible RH400.

O&K's RH200 excavator, introduced in 1989, weighed in at a healthy 529 tons. With the success of that model, the company set its sights on a much larger machine. As the world population of 240-ton-capacity haulers continued to increase in strength in the mining

Starting in June 1997, assembly began on the prototype RH400 at the Dortmund plant yard, in preparation for its unveiling to the mining press in July. The main boom assembly, with its TriPower linkage in place, weighs approximately 132 tons. *Terex Mining*

The size of the RH400's main boom is enormous by hydraulic excavator standards. Its complex shape, with its many rounded corners, is a bit more time consuming to manufacture, but its strength is unmatched in the industry. *Terex Mining*

industry, the company felt that it needed a hydraulic excavator capable of loading them in three passes. This machine was in the 40-cubic-meter bucket range, which led O&K to choose the model name RH400. All the company needed now was a customer for such a unit. That customer was found in northern Alberta.

The operations of Syncrude Canada, Ltd., which mines oil sands, sometimes referred to as tar sands, are

located just north of Fort McMurray, Alberta. The Athabasca Oil Sands Deposit of northern Alberta, which is approximately twice the size of Lake Ontario, plus Alberta's three other oil sand deposits, contain almost five times more oil than the conventional oil reserves of Saudi Arabia. But the oil is locked in a mixture of sand, bitumen, mineral-rich clays, and water. Though the modern mining of oil sands has been going on for the last few decades, recent advancements in the size of mining shovels and haulers have swayed many of the operations in the area, including Syncrude, to increase the size of their big shovel-and-truck fleets, and move away from dragline and bucket wheel excavators. To meet planned expansions at Syncrude, including its new North and Aurora mine sites, larger shovels and trucks would have to be acquired. Because of Syncrude's positive experience with two previous O&K RH200 front shovels, the company thought that O&K's planned RH400 could be the high-production machine the company was looking for.

In 1995 Syncrude and O&K formed a cooperation committee that would make the RH400 a reality. Teams of engineers jointly developed key design areas of the new front shovel especially to meet the rigorous demands of digging in the oil sands. Special attention was paid to the bucket design, carbody, and hydraulic systems, which had to be able to operate around the clock during the region's incredibly brutal winter months. The RH400 would have to be the toughest and largest hydraulic front shovel ever designed for series production.

O&K designed and fabricated the RH400 at its Dortmund, Germany, facilities, home of the company's large mining excavators. Because of the long lead times, the designs for the patterns were built first. These would be required by the foundry for forming the molds for pouring the castings, such as those used in the undercarriage.

The undercarriage consists of the two crawler assemblies measuring 32 feet, 8 inches in length and 9 feet, 4 inches in height. The width of the track pads

With the boom in place, workers finish lowering the massive 12-ton cooling unit module into place on the RH400. The cooling unit is responsible for keeping the machine's hydraulic fluid temperature in check. *Terex Mining*

is over 6 feet, with each cast pad made out of high alloy steel. The track pad and chain link are combined in a single unit for maximum strength and durability. Each crawler assembly is driven by a single three-stage planetary drive transmission, powered by two two-stage hydraulic motors. Each of these planetary drives weighs approximately 13 tons and are some of the largest built in the industry. For comparison, the massive electric-powered planetary propel units on a P&H 4100 series shovel weigh only 11 tons. The torque rating for the

RH400 planetary drives is a whopping 1,474,600 ft-lb. Top speed is a blistering 1.37 miles per hour.

The crawler assemblies are mounted to the carbody, which also acts as the base for the slew, or swing ring. This is the revolving structure that the superstructure frame will be mounted to. This frame is the single largest fabrication on the RH400. This structure will support the rest of the upper works, including the engine module, hydraulic and fuel tanks, and operator's platform. Steel plating for the superstructure was cut using an NC (numerical control)

As the RH400 nears completion, the tracks are soon pulled into position around the crawler frames and the hydraulic planetary drives, which weigh more than 13 tons each. Each crawler belt weighs approximately 64 tons, and each crawler assembly measures 32 feet, 8 inches in length. *Terex Mining*

oxygen cutting machine, with the aid of a camera-controlled robot. After all the steel plates are welded together, full ultrasonic test inspections are performed on all the joined pieces, to ensure that not even the tiniest weak weld joint escapes detection. This process is performed on all critical welded areas throughout the machine.

Mounted at the rear of the superstructure is the engine module. This structure contains the RH400's two diesel engines and the hydraulic and electrical components. The engines are mounted side by side in their individual compartments, separated by the main hydraulic tank. The mountings for the engines are on top of the main fuel tanks, whose capacity of 4,227 gallons of diesel fuel allows for 28 hours of operation between fill-ups. Each engine has four main hydraulic pumps attached to it for powering the main hoist and digging cylinders, and three hydraulic pumps for the swing drives. In all, there are eight main and six swing pumps. These pumps are the same units found on the tried and proven RH200 model. The radiators for the two engines are mounted at the rear of the module. But the cooling units for the hydraulic fluid are in their own separate module, which is mounted on the front right of the superstructure. Total weight of the engine module is 66 tons. The two-piece counterweight that attaches just behind the engine module weighs 88 tons.

The cab module mounts to the left front of the housing. The operator's compartment, along with the latest state-of-the-art controls and diagnostics systems, has an adjacent lunchroom with all the comforts of home, including clothes lockers, microwave, water dispenser, coffee machine, toaster oven, and a refrigerator. Air conditioning, a robust heater, and a stereo system are all standard fare. During long 12-hour shifts, often in remote areas of the mine, and especially during the winter months, these niceties become necessities for the operator of the RH400.

The digging front end of the RH400 comprises three main sections—the boom, the stick, and the bucket. The same care that goes into the fabrication of

The completed RH400, in July 1997, demonstrates its massive size by engulfing a 1962 vintage O&K RH5, the company's first fully hydraulic crawler excavator. This model type was originally introduced in 1961. *Terex Mining*

The 97-ton superstructure of the RH400 arrives in Fort McMurray, Alberta, Canada, in September 1997. The largest single structure of the excavator, it will mount on the carbody and slew ring and support all of the RH400's other component modules. *Syncrude Canada*

Workers prepare the slew ring area on the carbody for the mounting of the superstructure. Off to the left is the complete engine module with the Cummins diesel engines already installed. Weight of this unit is 60 tons. *Syncrude Canada*

the superstructure goes into the boom and stick. Cutting and bending all of the complex shapes results in tremendously rigid, close-welded box design structures. Once again, all welding seams are checked ultrasonically for the slightest defect. The main boom, which supports the massive TriPower linkage, weighs 132 tons. The main TriPower bearing pin alone weighs some 9 tons. This patented linkage design employed by O&K ensures automatic and constant-angle bucket guidance when crowding horizontally, or when raising or lowering the bucket attachment.

The business end of the RH400 is its 55-cubic-yard (42-cubic-meter), 80-ton-capacity bucket. No other hydraulic front shovel had ever been equipped with such a large bullclamas as the one found on the RH400. Previously, only large electric cable mining shovels were capable of handling such payloads. The main cutting lip of the bucket is a one-piece casting, utilizing seven digging teeth supplied by ESCO. The backwall of the unit is made up of more than 100 elements, providing an extremely strong structure.

The massive hydraulic cylinders, which provide all of the digging actions for the bucket, are designed and built by O&K at its Kissing plant. In terms of quality, these cylinders have few rivals in the industry. For instance, all of the seamless cylinder barrels are internally roller burnished to ensure extended service life of the piston rings. All cylinders also incorporate end-of-stroke cushioning on both the piston and rod ends, measurably improving service life. With some of the larger main hoist cylinders weighing 9 tons each, users want to get as much time out of these units as possible.

The 97-ton superstructure is lowered into place on top of the carbody. When attached to the slew ring, it will be able to rotate a full 360 degrees. *Syncrude Canada*

Most of the main components on the RH400 were produced by O&K, though some of the more specialized operations, such as the drop forging of the track rollers and large gear cutting, were subcontracted out to trusted allied manufacturers.

The engines on the prototype machine were two Cummins K2000E units, rated at 4,000 gross horsepower and 3,350 flywheel horsepower. From the beginning, these engines were meant as a stopgap only until Cummins was ready to release its new generation of Quantum QSK60 diesel units. The RH400 was designed to use the additional power of the QSK60 engines, but it would still be some months before the first of these engines would be

ready for excavator use. The original K2000E units would have to make do until then.

In July 1997, the prototype RH400 was officially unveiled at the Dortmund factory. In regular production series, the unit would never be completed to such a finished state. Instead, it would be shipped in its base component and module sections directly to the customer's mine site for final assembly. But because this was the first unit, additional procedures, including strain gauge testing, would need to be carried out on a fully functional machine. Also, officials from Syncrude would have to give the prototype the once-over and deem it ready for operations. After all preliminary factory testing was completed, the unit was dismantled and shipped in early August 1997 by sea to its new home in Canada. From start to finish, it took the O&K and Syncrude design teams only 18 months to make the RH400 a reality. Now it was time for the massive 910-ton hydraulic front shovel to show its new owners just what it could do.

The RH400 traveled across Canada on 12 rail cars as it made its way toward Edmonton. Arriving at the Clover Bar Rail Yards in mid-September 1997, it was unloaded onto a small army of semitrucks and trailers for its final leg of the trip up to Fort McMurray. Once on site at Syncrude, the RH400 was reassembled by the same O&K team from Germany in a record 10 days. By early October, the giant shovel was ready to taste oil sand overburden for the first time.

The RH400 (Syncrude Machine Number 11-35) was to be officially dedicated on October 22, with a symbolic "handing over of the keys." On October 23, the shovel was going to be put through her paces at the North Mine for all to witness. But a few days before the unveiling, the unthinkable happened. During loading testing, the shovel had an unexpected high-pressure hydraulic fluid filter failure, which compromised the oil going to the main hydraulic cylinders. Bits and pieces of the filter had contaminated the system and some of the cylinders. A failure like this was practically unheard of, but something would have to be done, and quickly, if the RH400 was to be ready for the unveiling. It was decided to fly two new spare cylinders from Germany into Fort McMurray via a C-130 transport. Two round trips were necessary to bring the spare parts in. Once in, service technicians would still need time to install the new cylinders. O&K already had some of its best people on the ground, but would they have enough time to make the necessary repairs? The unit did not have to work on October 22, but would need to be fully functional on the morning of October 23.

After the dedication, crews worked late into the night to get the RH400 on line. Come morning, chartered buses brought in the spectators. All witnessed the world's largest hydraulic shovel load 240-ton-capacity

Workers set the main pins that connect the hydraulic cylinders from the boom to the stick. These cylinders will provide the crowd force that applies the digging pressure of the bucket lip against the face wall. *Syncrude Canada*

Caterpillar 793B haulers with three very quick passes. After about 30 minutes of loading cycles, the buses were loaded back up, with only a few of the visitors knowing what had actually transpired during the previous days. Even though the shovel was operating, it was still not up to 100 percent. A final acceptance test required by Syncrude was delayed a few weeks while the RH400 was fully gone over with a fine-tooth comb. Finally, in December 1997, full Syncrude performance testing was carried out, with the shovel averaging 5,494 bank cubic

The welding of the high-tensile steel front bucket lip and the side walls into a single structure takes place inside one of Syncrude's work bays. Once finished, it will be connected to the bucket back wall, with ESCO tooth tips installed. Completed bucket structure weighs approximately 76 tons and is 18 feet, 2 inches wide. *Syncrude Canada*

yards an hour and 29 seconds per pass. The acceptance test was a complete success—so much so, that Syncrude approved the purchase of a second unit, which would eventually go on line in May 1998.

The second RH400 delivered (Number 11-36) was also equipped with Cummins K2000E diesel engines, but with a bit more grunt dialed in. These engines carried an output of 3,650 flywheel horsepower combined. By the end of 1998, the first machine would have its original engines removed and replaced with the new Cummins Quantum QSK60 units. Now the RH400 had the power to back up its prestigious bulk. The new engines were rated at a maximum 5,000 gross horsepower combined, but were only set up to deliver 4,000 flywheel horsepower. The rationale for the lower setting was to give the engines less stress to ensure a trouble-free life. At least that was the plan. Just a few hundred operating hours later, one of the Quantum diesels decided to go south for the winter. This engine failure took everyone by surprise. Even though the fault did not rest with O&K, Syncrude was disappointed with the setback. The engine was rebuilt and the first unit went back to work. But Syncrude decided that its next two RH400 shovels would not be equipped with the QSK60 diesels.

Shovels 11-37 and 11-38 would have significant alterations and improvements over the first two units. Changes were always part of the agenda with the RH400 program, since the first two units were essentially prototypes. O&K made changes to the bucket design, as well as the rest of the front end. These included a longer boom and stick to extend the shovel's overall working reach at the bench face. Also, new undercarriages, with wider tracks were installed to lessen the RH400's ground pressure weight. But the biggest change was the installation of two Caterpillar 3516B, 16-cylinder diesel engines, rated at a combined 4,600 gross horsepower and 4,400 flywheel horsepower. Now the RH400 had the power it always deserved. These changes brought the overall weight of the machine up to 965 tons. With fuel and hydraulic oil on board, the working weight is closer to 980 tons. The

third machine was put to work in April 2000, with the fourth following in May. These last two machines will make their homes at the Aurora Mine, while the first two will stay at the North Mine. During the year 2000, both of the first RH400 shovels will receive various engine modifications, as well as completely new undercarriages, bringing up both to the performance standards of the newest models. Because of the modular design of the RH400, these types of upgrades can go on almost indefinitely, keeping the shovels in front-line duty for years to come.

The first four RH400 excavators were purchased by Syncrude, but the fifth machine found itself going out to the western United States. In May 2000 it was shipped from the Dortmund factory to the Jacobs Ranch Coal Mine, located south of Gillette, Wyoming, in the Powder River Basin. Unique to this unit, identified as the RH400E, is that it is electric powered, just like a cable shovel. The Jacobs Ranch Mine also operates an O&K RH200. The RH400E will go into service at the mine in July 2000.

When the RH400 was first conceived, O&K Mining GmbH was part of Orenstein & Koppel Aktiengesellschaft. Orenstein & Koppel AG operations, based in Berlin, centered around the production of construction equipment. O&K in turn was a business unit of Fried Krupp AG Hoesch-Krupp of Germany. In December 1997, O&K announced that it was selling its mining division to Terex Mining Equipment, Inc., part of Terex Corporation. In early 1998, the deal was finalized and O&K Mining was integrated into a newly formed division, Terex Mining, headquartered in Tulsa, Oklahoma. This group, which is also the home of Unit Rig trucks, is responsible for the sale and support of O&K mining excavators. O&K AG was not part of this deal, and in November 1998 was sold to New Holland N.V., of which the Fiat Group of Italy is the majority owner. Other than a change in corporate colors, which are now white with red trim, things are much as they were. All RH400 excavators are still built in Dortmund, as are all of the other O&K mining machines. The company is

The completed O&K RH400 in all its glory. Carrying Syncrude Machine Number 11-35, this unit weighed 910 tons, equipped with a 55-cubic-yard (42-cubic-meter) bucket. The RH400s placed in April and May 2000, Syncrude Machines 11-37 and 11-38, are equipped with slightly larger 57-cubic-yard (43.5-cubic-meter) buckets, which are matched to the newer machine's greater digging capabilities.

still referred to as O&K Mining GmbH, but now the parent company is Terex, instead of Fried Krupp.

When the mining market considers hydraulic shovels such as the RH400, what are its advantages and disadvantages compared to the well-established cable-shovel offerings? In the plus column for the hydraulic machines are their greater mobility, greater selective digging capabilities, and lower initial price. The cost of an RH400 is right around $7 million, while some of the largest cable machines are in the neighborhood of $10 million. Large cable machines often last well over 100,000 hours of operation, while large hydraulic machines' life spans are approximately 60,000 hours. When it comes to size, the cable machine wins hands down. Even though the RH400's payload capacity of 80 tons is huge, the cable machines' are greater still. The latest offerings from these manufacturers, such as the P&H 4100XPB and the Bucyrus 495-BII, are 100-ton-capacity shovels. Basically, if your mining operation is projected to have a short life, then the hydraulic machine makes perfect sense. But if the mine plan calls for a much longer life span, the larger cable machine seems to make the greater economic sense. Often, it is a mixture of the two types of loading shovels that make the best production sense. As an example, Syncrude uses both the RH400 and the P&H 4100 TS cable shovel at both its North and Aurora mine sites. The selective digging nature of the RH400 makes it a highly versatile loading tool. But when all-out, high-volume loading of oil sand is required, it's hard to argue with the productivity and range that are the trademarks of the 4100 TS and its 100-ton-capacity dipper.

At the time of this writing, the RH400, weighing in at 965 tons, is still the world's largest hydraulic excavator. Its closest rival is the Komatsu-Demag H740 OS, operated by Klemke Mining. Klemke does overburden removal for the oil sand operations, especially Syncrude, so the big Komatsu-Demag is never very far away from one of the RH400s. The H740 OS carries a 52.3-cubic-yard bucket and weighs in at 815 tons. It is even powered by the same Cat 3516B engines, though limited to 4,400 gross horse-

The RH400 is capable of loading 240-ton-capacity haulers, such as this Caterpillar 793B, in three quick passes, with a cycle time of 29 seconds per pass. Bucket payload capacity is just over 80 tons per bite. Maximum digging height of the first RH400 is 53 feet, 10 inches, with a maximum digging reach of 57 feet, 5 inches.

power and 4,000 flywheel horsepower. This shovel was an outgrowth of the H655S program, which weighed 755 tons, but now that Komatsu owns the entire Demag model line of mining excavators outright, its nomenclature was changed in January 2000, to the Komatsu PC8000. Only one H740 OS has been built, and it has been working for Klemke since January 1999.

Other possible rivals to the RH400 in the marketplace are the 633-ton Liebherr R996, and the 570-ton Hitachi EX-5500. Both of these machines, however, are quite a bit smaller than the O&K behemoth. Currently, Komatsu, Liebherr, and Hitachi all have bigger hydraulic shovels in the works, larger than the models they are currently offering. But will they be as large as the mighty RH400? Only time will tell.

MILWAUKEE'S FINEST
THE P&H 4100 LOADING SHOVEL

Milwaukee, Wisconsin, has for decades been associated with fine beer, thundering motorcycles, and the occasionally memorable baseball game. But few would ever guess that the Milwaukee area is also the mining shovel capital of the world. The city is the home of P&H Mining Equipment, which is part of Harnischfeger Industries. And just across town, in the suburb of South Milwaukee, is the world headquarters of Bucyrus International, formerly of Bucyrus-Erie fame. These two companies were in competition for most of the twentieth century and are still at it. Today, both companies build massive electric-powered, cable mining shovels, drills, and draglines. If you are a mining customer looking for big high-production loading shovels, then chances are very good you have both of these manufacturers bidding for your business. The stakes can be very high. The cost of the largest cable mining shovels ranges from $8 to $10 million each, with the largest draglines, in the 160-cubic-yard range, in excess of $60 million!

During the last few years, one shovel has dominated the large open-pit mining sector. That machine is the incredible P&H 4100 series, built by Harnischfeger. Developed in the late 1980s and officially released in 1991, it was sized to load the largest category of haulers at the time, the 240-ton-capacity class, in three quick passes.

To build a shovel like the 4100 series takes years of design and manufacturing know-how. Harnischfeger was established in 1884, as the firm of Pawling & Harnischfeger, Engineers and Machinists. The company's first true success came in building industrial overhead electric cranes. To help diversify the firm's offerings, excavating equipment was slowly introduced, starting around 1910 with several types of trenching machines. Then in 1918, it introduced the industry's first gasoline-powered 1 1/4-cubic-yard dragline. This was followed in 1919 by the company's first cable-type shovel, the Model 205. The Model 205 used a half-track type of undercarriage design with steel wheels and crawler belt assemblies combined. But it

The first P&H 4100 shovel was delivered into service in July 1991, at the Caballo Mine, just south of Gillette, Wyoming. Pictured here working in October 1998, it is now equipped with an offset operator's cab. It was delivered with a right-side unit mounted flush with the side of the main housing. *ECO collection*

Using the advanced CATIA v5, 3D imaging software and 4D Navigator, Harnischfeger engineers can create computer-generated three-dimensional images of literally every part on the new P&H 4100XPB, to check for fit, lines of sight, and the interaction of various component modules with one another. *P&H*

input to DC operating power. These large, tough, and highly productive shovels gave stiff competition to the likes of Bucyrus-Erie and Marion Power Shovel. Every 2800 series shovel sold, and there were a lot of them, meant a lost sale to one or the other manufacturer. The 4100 series did not replace the 2800 series; instead, it was the next rung up the ladder.

Since the release of the first 4100 unit in 1991, the shovel has been constantly improved and updated. Models and variations include the 4100, 4100A (1994), 4100A LR (1995), 4100 TS (1998), and the latest incarnation, the 4100XPB (2000). At the time of this writing, just over 100 of the 4100 series machines have been sold worldwide, making it the best-selling ultralarge, two-crawler mining shovel ever produced.

All of Harnischfeger's mining shovels, including the 4100, are designed and built at the company's West Milwaukee National Avenue plant. Engineers design these machines using sate-of-the-art computer modeling and finite element analysis (FEA) software programs. In the case of the latest design, the 4100XPB, the fifth generation of the CATIA 3D design software was used. CATIA (Computer-Aided Three-Dimensional Interactive Application) actually originated with Lockheed as a CAD-CAM 2D program. In 1975, the French aerospace manufacturer Avions Marcel Dassault (AMD) purchased the program from Lockheed to design its products. Since the original program was two-dimensional in nature, AMD improved it by recreating it in a 3D package. Developed in 1977, it was the first CAD (computer-aided design) program designed for 3D use. In 1981, AMD realized that other manufacturers were interested in its new software and created a new subsidiary company, Dassault Systemes, to address this new market. In 1982, it officially released CATIA v1 to the engineering design community. In 1992, IBM became the sole supplier of CATIA in the North American computer software market.

The CATIA software is able to create complex 3D models for a variety of engineering needs, including finite

was the release of the firm's first electric mining shovel, the 1200WL series in 1933, that really put its quarry and mining machines on the fast track. This model would lead to its very popular 1400 series in 1944. From then on, there was no looking back.

The 4100 series of large mining shovels was an outgrowth of the company's extremely popular 2800 series of machines introduced in 1969. The 2800 machines were also the first P&H shovels to be equipped with the company's Electrotorque system for converting AC electrical

At the P&H main fabrication and assembly plant in Milwaukee, Wisconsin, this Ransome welding manipulator, used with a Reed positioner (center), with a 250,000-pound capacity, handles heavy welding jobs. Here it works on a shovel carbody. *P&H*

A modern P&H mining shovel contains more than 50 large gears, ranging from several inches to more than 18 feet in diameter. The teeth of these gears must be hardened to withstand the shovel's hard work life. Different uses require different treatments. This outer rim of the gear shown is being hardened in a bath of molten salt. *P&H*

analysis. This powerful computer program ensures that all of the 4100XPB shovel's many assemblies fit together perfectly, eliminating the need for in-plant preassembly before shipping. CATIA helps in the production of castings, in that the design can be translated directly from the solid 3D model, to FEA, then to pattern-making, saving tremendous amounts of manufacturing time. To visually be able to "fly" through these computer models, the 4D Navigator design tool is used. By being able to fly through the 3D models, engineers are able to verify such aspects as clearances, accessibility, and lines of sight, all before one piece of metal is cut or machined. Harnischfeger engineers used all aspects of the CATIA 3D design program to create the 55 major component modules that make up the new 4100XPB.

The manufacturing stage for a P&H shovel at the main plant consists of seven key steps: flame cutting, processing, welding, machining, heat treating, assembling, and finishing. Steel for a shovel takes two primary routes through the plant—structures and fabrications, and gears and mechanical parts. All electrical motors and components are P&H designed and built, except a few that are jointly produced by P&H and General Electric.

The 4100 series shovels, like others built by the company, never reach final assembly at the plant. Instead, component assemblies are only partially put together on the machine deck on the main shop floor. It takes just a bit of imagination to visualize what the shovel will look like in all of its modular component fabrications. All major structures, such as the crawler frames, track sections, boom, and bucket, are shipped individually. Only after it arrives at its ultimate destination is the shovel fully assembled. It takes from five to six months from the time the shovel is ordered, to the time it leaves the factory in some 7 railroad cars and 22 flatbed trucks.

Because of the advanced computer design work incorporated into the latest 4100XPB, the modular component sections are built in such a way that very few need to be fitted together at the plant. In the past, one could recognize

Here the crawler frame rail of a P&H 4100 shovel is being welded together by skilled company welders. Though many of the large structures are welded by automated machines, building cable shovels of this size is still basically a hands-on endeavor. *P&H*

This massive crawler frame rail is for the latest 4100XPB shovel and is nearing final completion. When the track pad links are finally mounted on the crawler frame, it will measure 38 feet, 6 inches in length. *P&H*

the machinery deck taking shape on a shovel. But with the 4100XPB, module sections, such as the boom, revolving frame, dipper handle, bucket, and transformers, are built to a finished state and then customized to fit a customer's exact requirements. Each of these modules is sized for easy shipping by rail or truck. The benefits of this manufacturing technique include shorter lead times, quicker assembly, easier exchange of units later in the shovel's life, reduced delivery time, and accurate module fit, requiring less welding in the field.

In April 1991, Harnischfeger shipped its first 4100 series shovel, to the Caballo Mine near Gillette, Wyoming. This coal mine was owned at the time of delivery by the Carter Mining Company. Today, it is the property of the Powder River Coal Company, which is part of Peabody, headquartered in St. Louis, Missouri. After field assembly, the first 4100 started digging in July 1991. This first machine was equipped with a 59-cubic-yard dipper capable of handling an 85-ton payload. Initially, the shovel was matched to the mine's existing fleet of 170-ton Unit Rig Mark 36 haulers. But the mine shortly brought in new Caterpillar 240-ton-capacity 793 haulers, which were a better match for the big shovel. The 4100 could load the 240-ton trucks in three quick passes each. Only two very careful dipper passes were needed for the smaller 170-tonners. This first shovel also featured a right-side, flush-mounted cab design. After the first few of these shovels were manufactured, P&H redesigned the unit so the cab would overhang on the right side of the housing, giving the operator a wider, more unobstructed view of the loading area. When the first 4100 underwent some scheduled maintenance to its undercarriage, it was retrofitted with an offset cab.

Unlike automobile and truck assembly line production, which is classified by model year designations, mining shovels, such as the 4100, have no particular model year assigned to them. When upgrades are made during the manufacturing of newer machines, these improvements are quite often made to the machines already in the field. Just about any part or major assembly can be

With the CATIA v5 software, each component, whether in separate pieces, or as a complete assembly—such as this 67-cubic-yard dipper for a 4100XPB shovel—can be rotated and manipulated in endless ways. Using the 4D Navigator tools, you can even "fly" through the bucket itself, as well as every other assembly on the shovel. The great versatility of the software gives engineers a complete perspective of the design process, allowing them to make crucial weight and strength estimates with great accuracy. *P&H*

From computer programs to reality—a 4100XPB dipper comes together on the shop floor. This P&H Optima bucket is rated at 67 cubic yards, capable of handling a 100-ton plus payload. *P&H*

retrofitted at the mine site to bring that shovel up to current model performance standards. This can keep your shovel productive for decades of hard rock digging use.

When the 4100 series was introduced, overall working weight of the shovel was around 1,175 tons, which included 165 tons of metal punchings supplied by the customer to act as counterweight. This is loaded into the rear of the shovel during final field erection. By the time the improved 4100A model was introduced in 1994, working weight had increased to 1,314 tons. As the shovel evolved and was improved during the 1990s, the weight of the shovel increased accordingly. The 4100A made the offset cab standard fare, as well as a longer boom, now 64 feet, compared to the original 60-foot version. This increased the overall working range measurably. The twin rectangular dipper handles were also increased in thickness for extra strength and stability during the digging cycle. The 4100 shovel was a good machine. The 4100A was a great machine.

During the run of the 4100A series, a few special versions were designed and built for customers with very specific needs. In 1995, P&H delivered a long-range coal loading shovel called the 4100A LR. Built for Powder River Coal Company's North Antelope Mine (now North Antelope Rochelle Complex) in the Powder River Basin (PRB) of Wyoming, it was equipped with a special 80-foot boom for increased working range and height. The dipper on the LR was a massive 80-cubic-yard coal loading bucket, the largest ever fabricated by the company. Overall working weight of this unit is 1,366 tons. Currently, only one of these has been built.

An even more specialized shovel, identified as the 4100TS, was developed for use in the oil-sands mining area north of Fort McMurray, in northern Alberta. The 4100TS shovel is designed with superwide 138-inch crawler shoes, which provide the needed flotation for the shovel's hefty 1,489 tons of bulk on the soft ground conditions found during the spring and summer. Special attention has also been paid to the design of the front end of the

The dimensions of the P&H 4100A dwarf all other equipment at the mine site. Shovels of this size only take a back seat to the ultralarge stripping machines and giant bucket wheel excavators. The 4100A measures 32 feet wide at the crawlers and 43 feet overall. From ground level to operator eye level is 32 feet. Height to the top of the main housing is 27 feet, 6 inches. Crawlers are 38 feet long. Operating weight of this model of shovel is approximately 1,355 tons.

shovel to cope with the extremely tough winter frost digging conditions. Additional cutting force is delivered to the dipper lip, and the bucket features extra wear protection, helping it survive the extremely abrasive material it digs.

The first 4100TS shovel was shipped from the P&H plant in July 1998, destined for Suncor Energy. It was commissioned in October of that year. This shovel was equipped with a 58-cubic-yard dipper, rated with a 100-ton payload capacity, on a 70-foot boom. In May 1999,

This shovel is the P&H 4100A LR (Long Range). Built for the North Antelope Mine (now North Antelope Rochelle Complex) near Wright, Wyoming, it is equipped with an 80-foot boom length, which allows it to load high-side haulers with coal bodies. Its maximum digging radius is almost 94 feet. Only one 4100A LR has been built.

The business end of the P&H 4100A LR is its coal-loading dipper, which is rated at a whopping 80 cubic yards. It is the largest dipper ever fabricated by the company. This bucket is designed to dig and load only coal. *P&H*

Suncor's neighbor, Syncrude, took delivery of its first 4100TS shovel, with plans to match it to Caterpillar's new 360-plus-ton 797 hauler, on order at the time. At the time of this writing, Suncor operates two 4100TS shovels, while Syncrude has three on the ground, with a fourth one ordered in February 2000 and scheduled for delivery at the end of the year.

The advancements incorporated into the 4100TS would lay the groundwork for P&H's most technologically advanced shovel to date—the 4100XPB. The 4100XPB was designed to meet the mining industry's increased production output made possible by the new ultra-hauler class of trucks. This shovel is capable of loading 360- to 400-ton haulers in four quick passes. The shovel is rated with a nominal 67-cubic-yard dipper capable of 100-ton payloads. With this kind of capacity, extra attention was paid to the overall cycle times and how to keep them as low as possible. The 4100XPB uses three swing motors instead of the usual two, giving the shovel an average cycle time of 29 seconds—10 seconds to dig, 11 to swing to the

P&H'S OTHER BIG BOY—THE 5700

As advanced and large as the P&H 4100XPB is, it was not the largest two-crawler shovel built by Harnischfeger, at least as far as overall size is concerned. That honor goes to the shovels in the 5700 series, which are still considered the largest two-crawler shovels ever built in the world. Even though none of the five 5700 machines built ever carried a larger dipper than the current 4100XPB, its overall bulk made them the supreme loading shovels for their day. Only the giant super-stripping shovels of the 1950s and 1960s could humble the mighty P&H excavator.

The 5700 shovel series was first conceived in the 1970s as the principal loading tool of the new mega-haulers that were being developed and introduced by the truck manufacturers, particularly the General Motors Terex 33-19 Titan hauler. With the release of the Titan in 1974, its 350-ton payload capacity would usher in a new era of superlarge loading shovels. At least that's what P&H thought at the time. The fuel shortage crisis in the mid-1970s delayed the deployment of any more than one prototype 33-19 hauler. But P&H gambled on the economic times and proceeded with building its big shovel anyway. By the time the first unit was shipped from the factory in March 1978, the economy was starting to look more encouraging, especially in the mining of coal. But this was short-lived. The worldwide recession of the early 1980s, with its runaway inflation and double digit interest rates, put the 350-ton-capacity Titan project on ice permanently. The growth of mining operations slowed to such an extent that orders for new equipment reached all-time lows with almost all manufacturers in the industry. This, more than anything else, explains why only five of the massive 5700 machines were built.

The first of the giant two-crawler shovels was the 5700 LR. This shovel, which carried a 90-foot "long-range" boom, was destined for Arch of Illinois' Captain Mine, near Percy, Illinois. Nicknamed Big Don, after Don McCaw, the mine's long serving reclamation director, the shovel was officially dedicated into service on May 24, 1978. Painted "reclamation-green" and carrying a 25-cubic-yard bucket, it was the world's largest two-crawler shovel. It's

When the P&H 5700 LR was released in 1978, it was crowned the world's largest two-crawler loading shovel. And with an operating weight of 1,775 tons, no one was arguing the matter. The 5700 LR was originally delivered into service at Arch of Illinois' Captain Mine, near Percy, Illinois. Today, it makes its home at Arch's Ruffner Coal, in West Virginia. *P&H*

interesting to note that the Captain Mine was also the home of the 180-cubic-yard Marion 6360, the world's largest shovel of any kind. The 5700 LR weighed in at 1,775 tons and had a maximum working radius of 114 feet. In later years the shovel was repainted in a red-white-and-blue paint scheme. In December 1991, the shovel was moved from the Captain Mine to another Arch property, Ruffner Coal, located in West Virginia.

The second 5700 shovel was shipped from Harnischfeger's Milwaukee plant in January 1981, destined for Bloomfield Collieries'

Hunter Valley Mine in New South Wales, Australia. This machine was the first built as a standard-range unit, equipped with a 70-foot boom. Bucket capacity on this unit was 60 cubic yards, because of its shorter boom length. The main machinery deck and car body of this shovel pretty well mirrored the first 5700 LR machine. Overall working weight was up a bit to 1,838 tons.

The next 5700 unit to follow was the odd one of the group. Christened the Chicago, it was designed as a dredging unit, mounted on a large barge, minus its crawler carbody. Built in 1987 for Great Lakes Dredge & Dock Company of Oak Brook, Illinois, it was designed with two interchangeable front ends—a clamshell (grab) dredge and a dipper dredge. The clamshell front-end used three buckets, a 50-cubic-yard one for mud excavation, a 40-cubic-yard one for firmer material, and a 30-cubic-yard one for heavy-duty, hard digging. The dipper shovel front made do with two bucket sizes, 28 cubic yards for removing blasted rock and glacial till, and 18 cubic yards for digging unblasted rock and removing glacial till and boulders. It was the crown jewel of the Great Lakes dredging fleet. But the story of the Chicago does not have a happy ending. On October 5, 1996, while the barge was being moved to a new working location off the coast of Denmark, the Chicago was swamped by high waves 60 miles from the Esbjerg port. It then capsized and sank to the bottom of the North Sea. It was deemed too expensive to mount a salvage operation to bring her back to the surface.

The last two shovels built were both upgraded 5700XPA machines. Both of the 5700XPA shovels were virtually identical mechanical twins, with 70-foot booms and 57.5-cubic-yard dippers. These shovels were also equipped with massive planetary drives mounted on each crawler, replacing the previous carbody mounted motor and gearbox arrangements found on shovels one and two. The fourth unit was shipped from the factory in October 1990, to R. W. Miller & Company Pty., Ltd.'s Mount Thorley Mine near Newcastle, New South Wales, Australia, and was commissioned in early 1991. The fifth and last 5700XPA was shipped in January 1991, destined to Miller's parent company, Coal & Allied Industries' Hunter Valley Mine, also in New South Wales.

Of the five 5700 machines built, the fourth and fifth shovels produced, both 5700XPA models, were the absolute largest. The shovel working at R. W. Miller & Company Pty. Lid.'s Mount Thorley Mine and its sister machine at Coal & Allied Industries' Hunter Valley Mine, both in Australia, were virtually identical, except for paint. Each handled a 57.5-cubic-yard dipper and weighed a record 2,100 tons. *Harnischfeger*

It began full operations in July 1991. Each of these shovels weighed in at 2,100 tons fully operational, some 582 tons more than the current 4100XPB. Though the 5700XPA series was also offered with a 120-ton-capacity dipper option, none were ever put into service.

Today, the 5700XPA shovels still hold the record for the largest two-crawler shovels in the world, and both are fully operational. Though the 5700XPA is technically a discontinued model, if a customer really wanted one, P&H would be more than happy to build it. But P&H would much prefer you buy the 4100XPB instead.

Still another variation on the company's leading heavy mining shovel is the 4100TS, designed and built to work in the harsh conditions found in the oil sand mining area of northern Alberta. The first "TS" shovel was delivered in October 1998 for service with Suncor Energy. It has a 58-cubic-yard dipper rated at 100-ton capacity. The width of the crawler pads is a superwide 138 inches. These are necessary to support the machine's great weight of 1,489 tons on less-than-ideal ground conditions. *P&H*

truck and dump, and 8 to swing back to the bank. The previous 4100A averages 32.5 seconds. Tests of the first machine in February 2000, at Triton Coal's North Rochelle Mine in the PRB of Wyoming, produced cycle times as low 26 seconds! For a mining shovel weighing in at 1,518 tons, this is practically unheard of. If the 4100XPB were a car, it would be a Dodge Viper.

The controls in the 4100XPB are all new P&H Electrotorque Plus DC Digital Drives. The type found in the older 4100A series used an analog system, which required 16 different control cards on a per-motion basis. The new digital layout only uses five cards for the same functions. These controls also greatly increase the effectiveness and speed of diagnostics packages, which are both digital and software based. These advanced diagnostics systems allow the shovel to work not only faster, but smarter too. The end result is faster, more controlled operation of all working motions, including crowd, hoist, swing, and propel.

Other notable improvements include a raised boom foot and boom point for greater dipper clearance for loading ultra-haulers. Also, the crawlers are moved back for greater dipper clearance. All things considered, the 4100 XPB is the most advanced cable-shovel in the world today.

Across town in South Milwaukee, Bucyrus International has been feeling the heat from the P&H 4100 series of shovels. Bucyrus builds the very competent 495-BI, and the 595-B, which was formerly known as the Marion 351-M. Both models are 85-ton payload machines, but as the 1990s came to an end, the 4100 series shovels have outsold the Bucyrus machines almost three to one. With the introduction of the 4100XPB, both of the Bucyrus offerings are simply out-gunned. But Bucyrus is not a company that gives up so easily. At the end of April 2000, the company officially announced the development of a new 100-ton-capacity shovel, identified as the 495-BII. Bucyrus hopes to have the first one in-the-iron by the end of 2000 or the first quarter of 2001. The 4100XPB has drawn a line in the sand, and it will be up to the 495-BII to take the fight to the reigning champion. Let the digging begin.

Big and brawny, the P&H 4100XPB is as good as it gets for big cable shovels. With its new DC digital drive, it is the fastest cycling, large mining shovel the company has ever put into the field. This first 4100XPB belongs to Triton Coal and works at its North Rochelle Coal Mine in the Powder River Basin of Wyoming. It is equipped with a 68-cubic-yard dipper, with a 100-ton-capacity. Overall working weight is 1,518 tons. Start-up for the shovel was in February 2000. *P&H*

ONE STOUT SUPER-STRIPPER
THE BUCYRUS-ERIE 3850-B

There are big shovels, and then there are big shovels! The tracked loading and hydraulic shovels featured in the previous chapters are large machines in every sense of the word. But when compared to the majesty of a mighty super-stripper, their seemingly large girths simply fade away. With some towering 22 stories in the air, the super-strippers were supreme among shovel class earthmoving machines.

Most of the stripping shovels built in the twentieth century were manufactured by Bucyrus-Erie of South Milwaukee, Wisconsin, and Marion Power Shovel of Marion, Ohio. Of the ultralarge super-strippers, Bucyrus-Erie and Marion were responsible for all of them.

The stripping shovel's duties within a mining operation differ from that of a large crawler loading shovel. A loading shovel, whether of a cable or hydraulic configuration, is designed to load haulers. But a stripping shovel's lot in life was to uncover large coal seams by removing the earth, or overburden, as it is better known,

covering the rich mineral deposits. The stripping shovel actually travels on top of the coal seam, which it uncovers by digging ahead of itself. As the shovel digs, it deposits the material behind itself in large piles referred to as "spoil." As the coal is uncovered, other excavators, such as smaller loading shovels or large wheel loaders, load it from behind the shovel to various haulers. When the shovel reaches the end of the digging section, or "cut," it begins uncovering a parallel cut alongside the first, dumping the spoil in the areas where the coal deposits have been removed.

The first stripping shovel built is credited to Marion in 1911, with its steam-powered and rail-mounted Model 250. Other Marion firsts included the electric stripping shovel, the Model 271, in 1915; first crawler-mounted type, the Model 350, in 1925; and the first true super-stripper, the 5760 Mountaineer, in 1956.

Bucyrus was not far behind Marion when it offered its first stripping shovel in 1912, known as the 175-B.

Shown working in March 1972, the 3850-B Lot I shovel known as Big Hog, was the pride of the Peabody Sinclair Mine. Note the use of the improved oscillating crawler frame on the closest unit and the use of one of the original designs at the rear.
ECO Collection

It is the last week of December 1961, and the first major structures of the Bucyrus-Erie 3850-B Lot I shovel are starting to take shape. At this point, the lower frame box sections are welded together. Workers are putting the crawler assemblies together, including the leveling jacks. *Bucyrus*

Over the decades, the company had built many memorable machines. But in 1959, Bucyrus embarked on the design of a giant stripping shovel that was larger than anything the company had ever attempted to build before. It would be the world's largest mobile land machine. This super-stripper was called the 3850-B, and it would usher in a new era of ever larger ultralarge earthmoving machines in the 1960s.

The Bucyrus-Erie 3850-B started life in 1959, as a proposal for Peabody Coal Company. Peabody was in the market for a super-stripper for its new Sinclair Mine, located near Drakesboro, in western Kentucky. Peabody needed massive coal production capability to meet the needs of the new Tennessee Valley Authority (TVA) Paradise Steam Station, the Sinclair Mine's main customer. After early analysis, it was determined that the 3850-B would have to be able to dig up to 100 feet of overburden on the level, and have the needed bucket capacity to strip over 3 million cubic yards of material per month. To meet these requirements, Bucyrus engineers established

By mid-January 1962, the 3850-B's crawlers are finished and are now able to support the weight of the lower framework. The swing rack has also been completed by this time. *Bucyrus*

The original solid frame crawlers of the 3850-B measured 40 feet in length and were 7 feet, 6 inches wide. Each two-track truck assembly was 22 feet, 6 inches wide. The track pads weigh 2 tons each, and there was a grand total of 296 of these for all eight units. *Bucyrus*

The massive 54-foot-diameter roller circle rail is installed by the last week of January. With its 100 flanged tapered rollers, it will support the entire weight of the revolving frame, as well as the rest of the upper works. The shovel's completed housing will eventually be able to rotate a full 360 degrees on these bearings. Each of these roller bearings was 18 inches in diameter. The Lot II shovel used 80 22-inch bearings, though the diameter of the roller circle rail was unchanged. *ECO collection*

the shovel's main working capacities and range. It would have to have a bucket size of 115 cubic yards, be able to dump at a height of 150 feet, and have a dumping radius of 210 feet at maximum height. This would enable the shovel to dig at one point and deposit the material up to 420 feet away. With this information in hand, force and speed requirements could now be calculated. First, the loading on the main upper structural assemblies was made and an estimated weight established. This would then determine the load factor on the lower works, which included four complete crawler assemblies, with two tracked units each. Next followed the calculation of the bearing area needed to support the shovel on coal and the propelling force required to move such a machine. This established the size and spacing of the crawler assemblies, including track width.

The design specifications established were truly awesome for an earthmoving machine of its day. The 3850-B would weigh in at roughly 9,000 tons with ballast, which acts as a counterweight when the shovel is in a swinging motion. The top of the boom was some 213 feet in the air. Length of the boom was 210 feet. Overall width of the crawlers was 70 feet, 6 inches. There would be 52 electrical motors needed in various ranges to power all of the massive workings, totaling about 12,000 electrical horsepower. To put these dimensions to scale, the 3850-B was 90 feet taller than the Statue of Liberty, wider than an eight-lane highway, and required enough power in a day to serve a small city of approximately 15,000 people.

Peabody officials were impressed with the 3850-B proposal. And in February 1960, the purchase order was signed, sealing the deal that would now make the shovel a reality. But Bucyrus-Erie had no time to waste congratulating itself. The TVA powerplant for which the Sinclair Mine was to supply coal was scheduled to go on line in September 1962. Peabody needed the giant shovel quickly, and Bucyrus knew it. It was now time to start the manufacturing process.

The initial design of the 3850-B had taken into consideration the size of the machine tools available for the fabrication and building of the various sections of the shovel. The weight and the section sizes had to be considered carefully, in light of limitations in the shop, with transportation, and of the field cranes at the erection site. In addition to this, a means of raising the 900-ton boom assembly in the field had to be incorporated into the shovel itself. The major structures of the 3850-B were primarily heavy steel plates, joined together with deep, full-penetration welds, carried out, whenever possible, by semiautomatic welding machines.

By April 1962, the machinery deck is well underway, with most of the swing motors now in place. The massive A-frame girder structures have also been pinned into place and will be responsible for supporting the weight of the entire boom assembly. *ECO collection*

The massive 115-cubic-yard dipper of the first 3850-B shovel is shown here in early May 1962, at the Bucyrus-Erie South Milwaukee plant. It has been assembled loosely at this stage to check overall fit and alignment of the various pieces before shipping. *Bucyrus*

Because of the enormous size of stripping shovels, they are built in subsections. Components must be of a size that can be loaded on to railroad cars and shipped to the mine site. As different component assemblies are built, they are fitted together to test for compatibility, then broken back down and loaded for shipping. Unlike an automotive assembly line, where at the end of the process, a car drives off the line, a machine of this magnitude doesn't reach its final assembly stages until months of on-site field erection takes place. During the building of the 3850-B, a steady stream of rail cars flowed out of the South Milwaukee plant. It would take some 300 rail cars to eventually transport all of the shovel's large bits and pieces to the mine site.

While the building of the first 3850-B was underway, Peabody surprised the company by requesting another unit, this time for its River King Mine, near Freeburg, Illinois. This shovel, known as the 3850-B "Lot II" machine, was ordered in 1961, with delivery scheduled for 1964. Bucyrus-Erie would now be building two 3850-B shovels at the same time, but the design specifications for the Lot II shovel were a bit different from the original unit, now referred to as the Lot I machine. Cost of the second machine was just a bit more than the first, at around $10 million in 1961. Biggest design differences for the Lot I and Lot II shovels were bucket capacity, 115 cubic yards vs. 140 cubic yards; boom length, 210 feet vs. 200 feet; dumping radius, 210 feet compared to 192 feet; main hoist rope diameter, 3 inches compared to 3 1/4 inches; and overall working weight, 9,000 tons vs. 9,350 tons. What the Lot II shovel gave up in working range it more than made up for it with its greater capacity bucket.

The field assembly for both 3850-B shovels followed pretty much the same procedures. To prepare the site, an area was selected that had the necessary room and rail lines to accommodate the massive collection of components that would have to be organized for assembly. An erection site was then dug out below ground

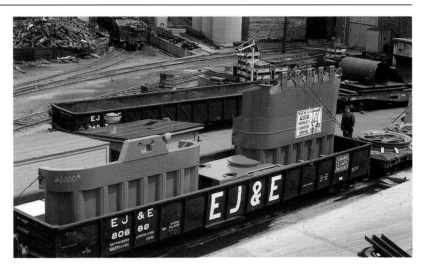

As the assembly continues on the giant shovel, the main hoist drums, gears, and motors are put in place in May. The 10-foot diameter drums are capable of handling 3-inch diameter hoist cable. The drum gears are 13 feet in diameter. Eight 625-horsepower DC mill electric motors power the hoist machinery, which are arranged symmetrically around the hoist drum. *ECO collection*

Once all the various sections of the dipper assembly were checked for fit, it was broken down into shippable sections, painted, and loaded onto railroad cars for the trip down to the Sinclair mine site in Kentucky. *Bucyrus*

level to about the ultimate height of the top of the lower works. This helped in the assembly process by splitting the difference between lowering components and lifting them. And since the shovel would have to dig its way to the mine site anyway (in the case of the Lot I machine, 3 miles), it would already be on firm footing and ready to go. A large derrick crane was erected just to one side of the shovel to perform the brunt of the lifting tasks, with the aid of various mobile auxiliary cranes on site.

The first steps in the assembly revolve around the heavy fabrications and framework of the lower works and the crawler units. The lower frame's deep box-section girders were assembled from 17 sections, supported on nested 8x8-inch wooden bracings and supports, referred to as cribbing. These support the massive weight of the steel structures while they were being welded together.

As this is being done, the crawler units were moved into place, along with the large hydraulic leveling jacks. Each crawler unit had two track assemblies, with each belt made up from 37 alloy steel pad castings weighing 2 tons each. There were 296 track pads in total. Width of the track pads was 7 feet, 6 inches. Each crawler belt was powered by 250-horsepower electrical AC motors, mounted two per crawler unit. Tractive effort of each crawler exceeds 600 tons. Each crawler unit was designed to support 1,500 tons, with the ability to withstand up to 3,500 tons under certain digging conditions. Each crawler unit was 22 feet, 6 inches wide and 40 feet long. Total ground bearing pressure exerted by the crawlers was 46 pounds per square inch.

The lower frame was supported on the crawler assemblies by four massive hydraulic leveling cylinders,

The massive saddle-block, weighing some 200 tons, served to support and cradle the dipper handle on the boom. The spring mechanisms helped combat the effects of inertia on the dipper handle while the shovel was swinging, and permitted 14 feet of movement sideways. *Bucyrus*

each 54 inches in diameter, with an 80-inch stroke. Each cylinder and piston unit weighed approximately 65 tons. During the shovel's digging cycle, signals received from a mercury leveling table opened and closed valves in the four cylinders, allowing hydraulic fluid to be pumped in at 3,000 psi, keeping the frame, and ultimately the shovel itself, in a horizontal position. Total hydraulic fluid needed for the leveling system was 4,500 gallons. Each hydraulic jack could handle 2,500 tons.

Once the crawlers were in place, the cribbing was removed, allowing the upper frame to lower itself on the jack supports to the fully down position. Once this was accomplished, the next step was to mount the swing rack and the 54-foot-diameter roller circle rail. There were 100 flanged tapered rollers mounted between the base and the bottom of the revolving frame. The revolving frame also acted as the base for the machinery deck. The rear section of the frame housed the ballast boxes, which would be filled with 1,250 tons of steel. Large cable reels were also mounted front and rear to take up slack in the electrical line powering the shovel.

With a solid base and revolving frame fully secured, various heavy-duty components were installed, such as the hoist machinery and multiple swing motor assemblies. There were six swing units, each powered by a 500-horsepower DC electric motor. These were responsible for accelerating and decelerating the revolving mass of the shovel. The massive A-frame girder structures were also mounted to the revolving frame and were held in place by large steel pins. This framework would form the structural gantry of the shovel and would ultimately be responsible for holding up the boom. Once the A-frame was in place, workers would put the framework for the house siding into place.

As work continued on the various elements inside the housing, the massive boom was carefully raised into position and attached to the A-frame by cables, and by two steel box girder beams, referred to as boom struts. These extend down from the top of the A-frame and

By May 1962, the massive dipper handle was at the mine site, awaiting arrival of the various sections of the dipper. The handle was 134 feet long and 7 feet in diameter, with 3-inch-thick walls made of high-impact nickel steel. It would eventually be mounted in the 40-foot-long saddle-block. *Bucyrus*

By June the 3850-B's housing is almost fully enclosed. Note the size of the shovel's superstructure compared to that of the semitank trailer truck parked between its crawlers, most likely delivering hydraulic fluid. *ECO collection*

mount midpoint on the boom, where the saddle-block would be mounted. The saddle-block, which weighed 200 tons, puts a massive strain on the boom and was responsible for supporting the dipper handle. The saddle-block measured 40 feet long and contained 32 heavy-duty 100,000-pound-capacity springs. The springs permitted 14 feet of handle and dipper movement sideways, helping to combat the effects of inertia, as the shovel revolved and decelerated.

After the boom was raised, the hollow dipper handle, with the dipper attached, was hoisted into place with the help of the shovel's boom and main hoist ropes acting as a crane. The dipper handle was 7 feet in diameter and 3 inches thick and measured 134 feet in length. It was made of high-impact nickel steel. Attached to the handle was the massive 115-cubic-yard dipper, fabricated in three large sections. The 16-foot-wide lip was an alloy steel casting, which at the time was the largest one-piece casting made in the company's history. The weight of the bucket lip alone was just over 18 tons. The dipper had seven digging teeth with renewable cap ends, which weighed in at 500 pounds each. With the dipper attached, total length of the handle was 180 feet.

While the dipper handle was being hoisted into place, workers were already painting the outside of the housing. Once the rope-crowd mechanisms were mounted on the dipper handle and the main hoist ropes connected to the bucket assembly, painters swung into full action, applying the final coats of Peabody yellow beige and green.

It was now August 1962, and after 11 months of field assembly the 3850-B Lot I shovel was ready for dedication. After its 3-mile journey to the mine site (top speed

Assembly of the main 115-cubic-yard dipper starts to take place in early August. The dipper was made of low-alloy, high-tensile steel plate, while the lip was a single cast alloy steel piece. The massive 16-foot-wide dipper lip alone weighed 18 tons. All tooth points were renewable, with replacement caps weighing 500 pounds each. *Bucyrus*

was 1/4 mile per hour), the mighty Big Hog—named by the workers at the Sinclair Mine—started to work. Like all super-strippers, the 3850-B used only electric power. It received this current via a 5-inch-diameter trailing cable, which supplied 7,200 volts to the shovel's generators. You would think a shovel the size of Big Hog would make quite a lot of noise. In fact, shovels of this magnitude are actually fairly quiet on the outside. About the loudest

thing a person hears from ground level is the sound of the blower fans circulating air through the housing as the shovel swings its backside in one's direction. These blowers were capable of forcing 500,000 cubic feet of air per minute, keeping the internal housing's temperature within acceptable levels.

Two years after the 3850-B Lot I shovel went to work, its sister machine at the River King Mine, took

The completed dipper and handle structure, which measures approximately 180 feet in length, is seen here in August, being lifted into position in the saddle-block. The 210-foot long boom of the shovel was raised at the end of July. *Bucyrus*

The giant leveling hydraulic struts of the 3850-B must support the shovel's weight and keep it in a level working stance, even when working on uneven ground. Each cylinder was 54 inches in diameter and had an operating stroke of 80 inches. The cylinders themselves weighed 35 tons each, while the pistons, with cast steel ends, each weighed 30 tons. Maximum capacity of each cylinder was 2,500 tons. *Bucyrus*

Workers make the final connections and adjustments of the bucket's hinged door tripping latch mechanism, which is operated by an enclosed ball bearing motor mounted on the dipper handle. It is controlled by a thumb latch switch located on the crowd master controller in the operator's cab. *ECO collection*

The interior of the completed machinery deck of the 3850-B shows the four-person elevator mounted in the center, with the swing motors to the right and left. The elevator traveled through the machine's center pintle from the lower works to the main machinery deck. It did not go all the way down to ground level. *Bucyrus*

its first scoop of earth on August 13, 1964. Because of the Lot II shovel's larger-capacity 140-cubic-yard dipper, it would inherit the title of the world's largest mobile land machine from the Lot I machine. Unlike the Lot I shovel, the Lot II 3850-B never really picked up a permanent nickname. It was sometimes referred to as the River King, though the name never stuck like Big Hog.

Not long after the shovels were fully operational, it became evident that a redesign of the crawler assemblies on both 3850-B shovels was in order. To solve premature frame failures, new units were designed with oscillating track bogie assemblies, which improved the reliability of the crawler units on uneven footing. Bucyrus first began work on the Lot II shovel's crawler frames in June 1967. These would be finished by the

The mighty and proud-looking 3850-B Lot I shovel takes a huge 115-cubic-yard bite of overburden at the Sinclair Mine in June 1964. The three round vents found on the forward sections of the outside housing were not part of the shovel's original design, but were added later to increase airflow within the machinery housing. There are an additional three on the opposite side of the machine. *ECO collection*

Looking much like its little brother, the 3850-B Lot II shovel had a slightly smaller working range and a shorter 200-foot boom. But its dipper was a mighty 140 cubic yards in capacity, compared to the Lot I shovel's 115 cubic yards. The three round air circulation vents seen on the forward left of the housing were there from day one. Only the first shovel was retrofitted with these in the field. The Lot II shovel officially started operations at the Peabody River King Mine on August 13, 1964. *ECO collection*

The massive dipper of the 3850-B Lot II shovel demonstrates just what 210 tons of overburden looks like. Its 140-cubic-yard capacity was second only to the simply huge 180-cubic-yard unit found on the Marion 6360, which could hold in excess of 270 tons. *Bucyrus*

The 3850-B Lot II shovel's only real rival was the incredible Marion 6360, nicknamed the Captain. Weighing in at close to 15,000 tons, it was the world's largest mobile land machine. The 3850-B Lot II machine tipped the scales at only 9,350 tons. The Marion behemoth is pictured working at the Captain Mine in November 1984. *Arch*

end of the year. The company began design work on the Lot I machine's new crawlers in May 1968. These were finished by the end of that year.

The reign of the 3850-B Lot II shovel as the world's largest mobile land machine would be brief. In October 1965, Southwestern Illinois Coal Corporation put its new Marion 6360 shovel to work at its Captain Mine, near Percy, Illinois. This was only about an hour's drive from where the big Bucyrus-Erie Lot II machine worked. The 3850-B Lot II machine, with its 140-cubic-yard capacity and its 9,350-ton operating weight, was a big shovel. But the Marion 6360 was bigger still. Its dipper size was an amazing 180 cubic yards, capable of handling 270 tons, compared to the 3850-B shovel's 210 tons. Marion's monster, nicknamed The Captain, weighed in at close to 15,000 tons in full operating trim. Even today, the Marion 6360 is considered one of the heaviest mobile land machines, if not the heaviest, ever to crawl on the face of the earth.

But the era of the giant stripping shovel would be a short one. As technology improved, the capacity of the shovel's closest rival, the walking dragline, soon equaled, then surpassed that of the stripping shovel. By the end of the 1960s, the walking dragline would reign supreme. In October 1971, the last stripping shovel built, a 105-cubic-yard Marion 5900, went to work for AMAX Coal Company's Leahy Mine in southern Illinois.

But if a mining company ever did want to make another stripping shovel purchase, how much would these monsters cost today? In today's dollar values, a shovel the size of the BE 3850-B would set you back approximately $77 million. And if you wanted one the size of the Marion 6360? Get ready to hand over a cool $120 million.

THE ULTIMATE WALKING DRAGLINE
BIG MUSKIE

When massive amounts of overburden must be removed economically, the giant walking dragline has been the mammoth mining machine of choice the world over for the last 30 years. It took decades for the dragline to catch up with the stripping shovel in range and capacity, and only a few years to surpass it.

The walking dragline gets its name from the method of locomotion employed by the machine. To move, the dragline lowers two long skids, or feet, picks itself up, and repositions, or walks, itself a few yards at a time. The innovation for this design dates back to 1913, when Oscar J. Martinson, of the Monighan Machine Corporation, patented the first "walking" mechanism for dragline use, referred to as the Martinson Tractor.

Major producers of walking draglines over the years have included such companies as Page, Ransomes & Rapier, Marion Power Shovel, and Bucyrus-Erie. Bucyrus got into the dragline market in 1931, when it purchased a controlling interest in Monighan, forming the joint venture company of Bucyrus-Monighan. Just after World War II, in 1946, the Monighan company was officially merged into the Bucyrus-Erie organization.

Once walking draglines started to approach the size of the stripping shovels, their key design and working characteristics could be brought to bear in large coal mining operations. One of the dragline's biggest assets was its superior working range, when compared to the giant shovels. This greater working radius enabled the dragline to cast its loads into spoil piles much farther away from the actual digging area. And since the dragline works above ground, as opposed to the stripping shovel which works below ground level, it can place this material more selectively. The shovel could only dump the material behind itself in spoil piles that sometimes would slide back into the pit and damage the shovel. The dragline would not have to contend with this drawback. Though on the downside, if the dragline

Weighing in at close to 14,000 tons with its 220-cubic-yard bucket, Big Muskie was the world's largest single-bucket earth-moving machine. The Marion 6360 stripping shovel weighed more than the 4250-W, but it's the size of the bucket that counts. And here, the dragline had bested the mighty shovel by 40 cubic yards. *ECO collection*

Measuring 105 feet in diameter, the massive tub of the Bucyrus-Erie 4250-W Big Muskie nears completion at the Central Ohio Coal Company's assembly site in June 1967. Throughout the massive dragline's life, it would eventually use three tubs, and each replacement unit was a bit stronger and a little heavier than the previous one. *Bucyrus*

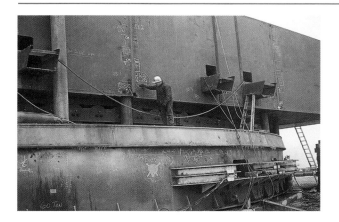

A worker standing on the outer rim of the tub is photographed in November 1967. The 90-foot diameter roller circle ring already is in place. Its 128 tapered bearings allow the revolving frame to rotate a full 360 degrees. In this image, the revolving frame has already been mounted. *ECO collection*

By February 1968, the first of the 4250-W dragline's 220-cubic-yard buckets was being tack welded together at Bucyrus-Erie's South Milwaukee plant to check for overall fit before being shipped down to the mine site in Ohio. *Bucyrus*

got too close to the edge, its working area, or bench, could break off and slide into the pit, taking the machine with it. Another deciding factor between the two types of machines is simply the geology of the working site. Where coal seams ran closer to the surface, especially in rocky conditions, the stripping shovel was the machine of choice. But as these relatively easy-to-reach deposits started to run out, mining operations had to dig deeper into the ground. The deeper the operation, the greater the handicap of the shovel's comparatively limited range. At a certain point, it just became more economical to keep the machine topside.

The first walking dragline to break the capacity barrier of 100 cubic yards was the Marion 8800. This machine originally went to work in 1961 at Peabody Coal Company's Homestead Mine in western Kentucky and was originally equipped with an 85-cubic-yard bucket. But not long after it went to work, it was replaced with the larger unit. Other notable large-capacity giants included the Marion 8900 series, of which two were built, one 130-cubic-yard machine and one 145-yarder. Both went to work in 1967. But these would soon seem puny in comparison to what Bucyrus-Erie had in mind. It was about to build the world's largest single-bucket digging machine. The title held by the mighty Captain shovel would soon be relinquished to a walking dragline by the name of Big Muskie.

The massive single steel casting of Big Muskie's digging lip measures 20 feet, 8 inches inside the lip opening and 23 feet outside across the entire piece. *Bucyrus*

In the early 1960s, Central Ohio Coal Company (COCC) of Cumberland, Ohio, a wholly owned subsidiary of American Electric Power (AEP), was in the market for a new high-capacity stripping machine to help meet the future demands of its primary customer, Ohio Power's Muskingum River Plant near Beverly, Ohio. COCC had been supplying coal to this power-plant since 1953. The plant was adding a fifth generating unit that would boost annual coal requirements from 3.2 million tons to 5.0 million. Company mining engineers estimated that there was less than 47.0 million tons of coal reserve left under 100 feet of ground cover. This was not nearly enough reserve for the Muskingum plant, let alone the Philo station, a customer to which COCC had been supplying coal since 1946. The mine was going to need a digging machine capable of uncovering coal deposits with overburden ranges of 160 feet, with some as deep as 200 feet. Another factor was the geological condition of the mining area. Much of this coal reserve lay in ridges with great irregularities, mak-

By June 1968, almost one year after the fabrication of the giant tub, the dragline's machinery deck on top of the revolving frame is beginning to take shape. One A-frame structure (on the left) is in place and the right is starting to be lifted into place. *Bucyrus*

The gigantic front cable sheaves of the 4250-W guide the 5-inch-diameter cable drag ropes into the main housing. Their over-and-under design helps keep the cables clear of the ground, where mud and debris picked up could damage the cable's inner pathways and drums. *Bucyrus*

ing the development of a satisfactory shovel pit almost impossible. These factors dictated a walking dragline.

The next question was how many draglines the company needed. Mining officials looked at the feasibility of two machines instead of one giant unit. Even though initially two machines would be slightly less expensive than one large one, the cost of operating and maintaining two active mining pits would quickly erase this advantage. The company decided on a single walking dragline with a bucket capacity of 220 cubic yards. A dragline of this size would also allow the company to retire a few of its older machines and still have the production capacity to meet all of the mine's output needs. In addition to the massive earthmoving capabilities of a dragline of this size, it would allow the company to mine the areas between the high walls left by contour mining operations. This would eliminate the high walls and help return the land to a productive postmining condition.

Both Bucyrus-Erie and Marion Power Shovel presented bids to COCC on its machine proposals. Bucyrus was officially given the go-ahead in 1966 to proceed with the fabrication and building of its design, the 4250-W. Since the mighty dragline would be working at COCC's Muskingum mining location, it picked up the nickname of Big Muskie. It would be referred to by this name for its entire working life.

Like the building of the 3850-B stripping shovels, the process of building and erecting the 4250-W for Bucyrus-Erie was, more than anything else, a logistical problem. One of the biggest differences in the field assembly of the 4250-W, compared to that of the stripping shovels, is that the entire erection process is done at ground level and not in an excavated pit area. But as with the giant shovels, a very large assembly area with rail line access and roads was a necessity at the mine site, or just off of it. When building a machine the size of the 4250-W, you needed all the room you can get. The measurement from the back of Big Muskie's hous-

This aerial shot of the 4250-W's assembly area in August 1968 shows the roof being installed on the main housing. The dragline's first two buckets and various sections of the main boom are also at the site. *Bucyrus*

In late September, both of the dragline's 155-foot masts were temporarily lifted into place. These structures, along with the A-frame gantry, would eventually support the weight of the 310-foot, twin-leg boom. *Bucyrus*

The main housing of Big Muskie was simply enormous and looked more like a warehouse than a machine. For scale, note the size of the worker as he crosses over part of the completed roof sections. The top of the house enclosure was 67 feet from ground level. Bucyrus

ing to the end of the boom in lowered form was 487 feet, 6 inches—more than 1-1/2 times the length of a football field!

Technological advancements since the building of Bucyrus-Erie's 3850-B Lot II shovel would help the company in the design and fabrication of such a behemoth. New and larger electrical motors and generators, along with more sophisticated control equipment, had been designed by outside suppliers. Also, new designs of wire rope, as well as advanced machine tools, had also been developed. All of these improved materials would play a role in building the giant.

At the mine site, an assembly area was prepared that would be the machine's birthplace and temporary home for the next several years during the building process. Auxiliary mobile cranes, as well as a large fixed derrick crane, would be needed to lift all of Big Muskie's bits and pieces into place. In 1967, field erection of the 4250-W officially commenced.

By June 1967, the base, or tub, that would support the massive weight of the dragline was well underway at the assembly site. Unlike a stripping shovel, which rests on four sets of crawlers with two track assemblies each, a walking dragline sits and rotates on a round tub. This

By early October, the first sections of the boom started to be put into place and supported by wooden cribbing, necessary to keep all the different sections in alignment during final welding procedures. *Bucyrus*

In another aerial view of the erection site, Muskie is shown in January 1969 with the boom's major sections all in place. It needed only a coat of paint. *Bucyrus*

base is connected to the dragline and is picked up each time the machine moves, or walks. The tub of the 4250-W arrived at the mine site in 31 concentric ring segments, ranging from 52 to 80 tons each. These sections were made up of carbon steel plates from 1/2 inch to 3 inches in thickness. More than 4,000 feet of field welding was required to join all of the sections together. Overall, the tub was 105 feet in diameter and 8 feet thick. The immense size of the base helped keep the ground bearing pressure of the dragline to 21 psi, which was far less than the 46 psi of the 3850-B stripping shovels.

Connected to the base was the revolving frame. This structure, as in the stripping shovel, would support the machinery deck and the A-frame steel structures for the gantry. The revolving frame, which was made up of 49 welded steel plate compartments, was supported on the tub by a 90-foot-diameter roller circle made up of 128 tapered and crowned steel rollers. Each of these rollers was 22 1/4 inches in length and 24 inches in diameter. Steel plate averaging 2 1/2 inches thick overlaid this frame, forming the machinery deck, to which all of the main drag, hoist, swing, power, and control machinery and equipment would be mounted. By November 1967, the revolving frame was fully in place on top of the massive tub.

During the next few months, rail cars continued to move large steel fabrications out of Bucyrus-Erie's South Milwaukee plant. The steel plates were being fitted into place for the first two of Big Muskie's buckets by February 1968. Once all of the fabrications were checked for fit, they were broken down and shipped to the mine site that April. They would be fully assembled on site by July 1968.

During the winter and spring months of 1968, great progress would be made on the 4250-W. By May, most of the 10 625-horsepower swing motors, responsible for revolving the machine on its base, were in place. The maximum swing torque produced by these motors was the equivalent of 225 tons of side load at the boom point. This torque resulted in the acceleration of the

Big Muskie's drag bucket was rated at 220 cubic yards and was capable of gulping 325 tons of earth and rock at a time. The empty bucket weight and all of its associated hardware totaled 230 tons. Exterior bucket height was approximately 14 feet, with an arch height of 22 feet, 9 inches. This arch design was converted in the mid-1970s from a single cable line to a twin-line layout. *Bucyrus*

bucket and its load from 0 to 15 miles per hour in approximately seven seconds. Other key assembly advancements made during this time were the installation of the massive front cable sheaves and their mountings, for guiding the 5-inch steel wire drag ropes, and the two walking platforms, or feet—though at this stage,

By January, the main walking system components, which were the dragline's only way of getting itself from point A to point B, were all in place. The walking shoes would support Muskie's massive weight as it moved backward in 14-foot cycle distances. *Bucyrus*

the feet were still not connected to the main housing by their hydraulic support cylinders. The A-frame girder structure and part of the housing side walls on the left side of the machine were now in place. By July, both A-frames would be in place, as well as all of the sides of the dragline. Also installed at this time were the blower motors, required to circulate no less than 1 million cubic feet of air per minute to keep all of the machinery housing ventilated. This was twice as much as the 3850-B shovels produced.

By August, most of the main housing was now closed in. The A-frame cross-supports were also mounted between the two main structures, completing the gantry. Two 155-foot tubular-framed masts were connected to the front end of the housing and temporally lifted into place in September. These masts, along with the A-frame structure, would support the massive twin-leg boom of Big Muskie with 3 5/8-inch-diameter wire rope bridge strands. There were 16 strands, 8 per side, connecting the A-frame to the masts. The boom was suspended by 12 strands, 6 per side, which were pinned to the two masts.

After the masts were in place, workers began fabricating the main boom. The boom structures were supported on wooden interlocked cribbing, to keep the sections on a level plane while they were welded together. The boom was made up of two separate rectangular columns, and joined together in the form of a V. Each column was built out of four 24-inch-diameter seamless steel tubes, laced together by smaller tubular sections for bracing. Heavy steel castings were used at each boom foot, as well as the boom end. When finished, the main boom would measure 310 feet in length, with a 110-foot width between columns at the boom foot of the dragline housing. Eventually, the boom superstructure would be filled with nitrogen gas to about 100 psi. A series of gauges would monitor this pressure and sound an alarm if it fell below a preset level, indicating a possible crack in the structure. This would then be tracked down by a sonic pickup. The boom on the 4250-W was a very robust design. It needed to be. The boom would have to be capable of carrying a suspended load of 550 tons. This is the average weight of the dragline's bucket and associated hardware fully loaded.

While the boom was being welded together, workers installed the massive hydraulic cylinders that attached the two walking shoes to the dragline itself. The shoes, which measured 130 feet in length, had a pivot joint in the middle, to take the stress off the structure when the full weight of the machine was applied on uneven ground. Each of the cylinders, two per side, were 58 inches in diameter. Mounted on the walking shoes themselves were four 27-inch diameter push cylinders, two per side, which would actually propel the giant. For Big Muskie to move, it would raise itself by lowering its walking shoes. This would raise the base of the machine several inches off of the ground. Then the dragline is pushed backward by the four push cylinders mounted on the shoes a total distance of 14 feet. Then the lift cylinders were retracted and the whole process began again. Top walking speed of the 4250-W, theoretically, was 900 feet per hour on a good day.

By October 1968, with a new winter coming on, the 4250-W's main boom was half assembled and painters were well underway painting the housing, revolving frame, and the two masts. The boom would finally be completed in January 1969. After it was painted a bright red, the mighty twin-leg structure was raised into the air for the very first time. This can be a very dangerous time in the early life of a dragline. If it isn't raised just so, motors can overload and burn out, not to mention the more general risks of damage created by the enormous stains on the superstructure. But once in place, all at the mine site breathed a giant sigh of relief. The boom went up with few hitches, all the way to its highest point, 222 feet from ground level. Now the 4250-W was starting to look like more than just some giant erector set. It was starting to look like the world's largest digging machine.

113

Muskie's boom was raised for the first time in late January 1969. To the relief of everyone at the assembly site, the boom went up without a hitch. Length from the back of the main housing to the end of the boom tip was 487 feet, 6 inches. *ECO collection*

The 4250-W finally got its less-formal name in March, when "BIG MUSKIE" was painted on both sides of the main housing. By the end of the month, Big Muskie's main 5-inch hoist and draglines had the first 220-cubic-yard bucket suspended in the air. And what a bucket it was. With a maximum width of 23 feet and length of 27 feet, 3 inches, it was as large as a 12-car garage. The bucket with its hardware weighed in at 230 tons empty and was capable of handling a 320- to 325-ton load in one scoop. Incredible. No other single bucket earthmoving machine was able to perform such a feat. The Marion 6360 Captain shovel came the closest, with its 180-cubic-yard dipper that weighed in at 165 tons empty, capable of a 270-ton bite per pass.

To handle a bucket the size Big Muskie swung, the 4250-W employed the largest hoist and drag cables ever produced. Each wire rope was 5 inches in diameter and weighed some 47 pounds a foot. Length of the four main drag ropes combined was 2,086 feet, with each having a rated breaking strength of 2,160,000 pounds. Two ropes on either side of the bucket were wound on 11-foot diameter drums, mounted in two independent, but electrically synchronized, machinery units. Power was supplied by eight 1,000-horsepower motors rated at 260 volts each, which developed the electrical equivalent of 22,000 horsepower at normal digging speeds. The four main hoist ropes that lifted the massive bucket had a combined length of 3,728 feet and carried the same performance specifications as the drag cables. Components for both the hoist and drag machinery units, such as the bearings, drums, gears, and pinions, were identical except for the intermediate gears, which were sized to secure suitable ratio changes. Ten 1,000-horsepower motors drove the hoist drums and generated a peak output of 27,500 horsepower during hoisting. If you were to add up all of Big Muskie's many electrical motors, such as generator, swing, hoist, drag, and so on, it would amount to a power output of a whopping 62,900 horsepower at peak power demand. Making all

Muskie's operators cab was mounted high off the ground on the right side of the front main housing. Located between the twin-boom structures, it gave the operators an unobstructed view of the bucket while digging and dumping. *ECO collection*

of this possible was a 4 7/8-inch, six-conductor trailing cable delivering 13,800 volts of electrical current into the machine. This cable was purchased in 2,000-foot sections, which were joined in the field by Westinghouse switch-houses.

Over the next few months, all of Muskie's components, systems, and motors were tested and retested to prepare it for full operational duty. On May 22, 1969, the Bucyrus-Erie 4250-W was officially dedicated into service. Almost a full two years of field assembly had been needed to put all of Muskie's bits and pieces into place, brought to the mine site on some 340 rail cars and 260 semitrucks.

It is hard to comprehend just how large a leviathan Muskie was. Since it didn't require crawlers to get around, it sort of resembled a large revolving warehouse with a boom on it. Its overall weight was greater than 150 Boeing 727 jetliners and with its great digging depth, it could have dug Lake Erie. Its working area was the equivalent of a 6-acre park. It was simply enormous.

Muskie's working credentials were impressive. Along with its mammoth bucket, the 4250-W had an impressive working range. It was able to dig in one location and deposit it some 610 feet away. It had a maximum digging depth of 185 feet. During the early design phase of the dragline in 1967, estimated overall working weight was quoted at 13,500 tons. But by the time everything was said and done, the weight ended up being more like 14,000 tons.

Keeping the dragline on line and in tip-top shape were four shift crews with seven employees each. Each crew had an operator, an oiler, an electrician, a welder, a general laborer, and two groundmen who operated the dozers for maintaining Muskie's working bench. But when a major repair, such as a tub or cable replacement was needed, the mine assigned as many workers to the task as needed. This was especially true during the two times that Muskie's tub had to be replaced. The original tub lasted until 1975. The second would take it to late 1982, when the third and last tub was installed. Work on this tub replacement finished up in early 1983. As each of these new tubs was installed, Muskie would put on a few pounds. Each tub was stronger and heavier than the preceding unit. This, along with various other structural upgrades, pushed the dragline's weight to an estimated 14,500 tons. To replace the 105-foot diameter base, it literally took every heavy-duty dozer and scraper outfit the mine could put to the task. Dozers such as Caterpillar D9Gs, Komatsu D455s, and Fiat-Allis 41-Bs, and scrapers units such as tandem-engined Cat 637s and big 657s would be brought to bear. It would take up to 36 or so machines in this size class to push and pull the old tub out from underneath it and replace it with the new one. It was truly a herculean task for the mine and its workers.

Muskie's place in earthmoving history is secure. No dragline ever really challenged the 4250-W for its crown. The closest contenders over the years have all been built by Bucyrus-Erie, which include two 3270-W draglines in 1979, rated at 176 cubic yards (both retired), and two 2570-WS units originally rated at 160 (currently 154) and 143 cubic yards, the latest of which just went to work in Australia in June 2000. Marion Power Shovel's largest factory-built dragline was the 8950 model of 1973, of which only one was made. Rated at only 150 cubic yards, it was considerably smaller than the 4250-W. The only larger capacity Marion dragline was the 8900, though not initially. Two of this model type were built in 1967, with the second unit equipped with a 145-cubic-yard bucket. But in 1993, Bucyrus, oddly enough, upgraded it to a 155-yard bucket. Sadly, it was parked in December 1999. Of all of these machines mentioned, only the 2570-WS draglines are currently in full operation.

Marion will never have the chance to build anything that could compete with Muskie. Bucyrus-Erie, whose name was changed to Bucyrus International in 1996, purchased the Marion Power Shovel Company in August 1997, ending the rivalry that had gone on

This view of the 4250-W's main machinery deck illustrates how just about every square foot of floorspace was occupied by one size of electric motor or another. Mounted in the center were the two main 11-foot-diameter hoist drums, with two 5-inch cable lines each. The main drag machinery and drums are located behind, to the right and left, of the main hoist drums. *ECO collection*

Bucyrus-Erie originally built two cable carriers to handle Big Muskie's hundreds of feet of 4 7/8-inch, six-conductor electrical trailing cable, which supplied 13,800 volts of current to the leviathan. But in reality, these cable reel carriers proved to be too cumbersome. Eventually, the mine developed its own method of moving the cables with nylon slings and bulldozers. *ECO collection*

The view from the main operator's cab was, to say the least, panoramic. Two levers and two pedals handled all of the dragline's major working motions. Just behind the operator's seat and to the left was a full-size refrigerator. There were also at least four extra chairs in the cab, so workers could take lunch and dinner breaks in the machine. *Bucyrus*

Watching Big Muskie tear a massive 325-ton bite of overburden out of the earth was truly an exciting experience. Big Muskie may not have been the heaviest earth-moving machine ever built by man, but without a doubt, it was the greatest. *ECO collection*

between the two companies for 113 years. Marion's product line was integrated into Bucyrus', as were many of the machine tools at the plant in Marion, Ohio. The old factory was emptied and the Marion name retired. Now all that remains is Bucyrus.

Over the years, there has always been some disagreement as to the meaning of "the world's largest" when speaking about Big Muskie and the super-strippers of old. Are we talking about capacity? Weight? Overall size? One does not necessarily mean the other. Muskie has often been referred to as the world's largest mobile land machine. Well, yes and no. When it comes to outright capacity, Muskie has no equal for a single-bucket digging machine. But when it comes to size, things get a bit more complicated. If we are referring to weight alone, this opens the door for the Marion 6360, and eight bucket wheel excavators (BWE) working at Rheinbraun lignite mines in Germany. Built by various German manufacturers over the years, including Buckau-Wolf, O&K, Krupp, and MAN/Takraf, these BWEs are simply gigantic and weigh in at between 13,367 for the earliest, to 14,877 tons for the latest. The largest of these are rated at 240,000 cubic meters daily output. Of the largest machines, Rheinbraun numbers BWE 285 and 287 are both 200,000-cubic-meter excavators, while BWE 288, 289, 290, 291, 292, and 293 are all 240,000-cubic-meter daily output giants. The Marion 6360 Captain shovel was originally specified at 14,000 tons during its early design phase. But the truer weight was right around 15,000 tons.

There just isn't any good way of verifying the largest or heaviest machine, but it is probably a safe bet that the Captain shovel, and the O&K BWE 292 and the MAN/Takraf BWE 293, each of which weighs in at approximately 14,877 tons, all outweigh Big Muskie. It seems most would give the nod to the Marion 6360 as being the heaviest mobile land machine ever built. But to miners, what really counts is the capacity of the bucket, and here all are in complete agreement—Big Muskie was the largest single-bucket earthmoving machine ever created.

EPILOGUE

June 1999. I was on my way down to the Central Ohio Coal Company to photograph a pair of Caterpillar D11R CD Carrydozers. But on this trip, I was not looking forward to being at the mine. I knew that the centerpiece of the coal mining operation, Big Muskie, was in the early stages of being dismantled and scrapped. Though tons of steel stood to be reclaimed and reused, it was hard to imagine the demise of the legendary mining machine.

After the work with the dozers was over, I asked permission to go over to the disassembly site, which was granted. Only a few miles from the main mine offices, the massive dragline had sat idle in the same place were it was parked on January 29, 1991, the official date of its decommissioning. I had been to this particular site two previous times to see Big Muskie in its idled condition. I wondered just how much of it was still left. Arriving at the site at about lunchtime, I surveyed the dismantling area. It looked as if some giant had taken a can opener to it. Not a very pretty sight.

Though a few groups tried desperately in the final months of Big Muskie's life to have the behemoth saved and preserved as a museum and tourist attraction, it was too little, too late. The company that had received the contract to dispose of the dragline, Mayer-Pollock Steel Corporation of Pottstown, Pennsylvania, actually had agreed to a cash buyout of its contract. But it was the $2 million that AEP wanted to free it from all present and future liability concerns that was the real issue. There just wasn't enough time to raise the money. The demolition company started work on Muskie in March 1999, even though negotiations were still taking place on a way to raise the funds.

All of that ended on May 20, 1999, when Dykon Explosive Demolition of Tulsa, Oklahoma, set off 20 pounds of explosive charges on the A-frame supports at roof level, severing the gantry supports, sending it and the

On May 20, 1999, Big Muskie's 310-foot boom was sent crashing to the ground. By June 4, almost the entire middle sections of it had already been cut up for scrap and hauled away. Most thought this fate would not befall such a giant as the 4250-W dragline. Its end is simply tragic and a loss for all future generations.

310-foot boom crashing down to the ground. Just 15 seconds later, it was all over. There was no turning back now. For a dragline, this step in the demolition process is a mortal blow. The end of the world's largest single bucket digging machine was at hand.

I thought to myself that it would have been better to photograph Muskie a few hours earlier, with the lower morning sun. She faced north, so the front of the machine was always in shadow. But this would have to do. I walked around the area, using two cameras, one for medium format images and another for 35-millimeter slides. Five-inch cable covered the ground like so much steel spaghetti. The center section was almost completely cut out of the main boom at this point. When the gantry was brought down by explosives, it also tore away much of the front end of the main housing. Toward the back of Muskie, an earthen ramp had been made leading up to and into the rear end of the main housing. This made it easier to remove all of the electric motors and various other components that formed the "guts" of the dragline. These had monetary value as they were, and customers would eventually be found. The rest of the metal structures would be cut up into transportable bits and pieces to be hauled off and eventually melted down.

After my walk around, I put the cameras away and took out a cold drink from the cooler. I stood in the hot sun, in tall grass on the right hillside overlooking Muskie, drinking my soda, thinking of the times that I had seen the 4250-W working. In her life, Muskie was a hard-working and pretty reliable machine. She had gone through numerous upgrades and structural reinforcements over her life but never had a major catastrophe.

I always thought Big Muskie would survive, in some form, into the twenty-first century. I once wrote that it would be unthinkable to let cutting torches have their way with her. I was wrong. Standing there, I knew this would be the last time I would see Muskie. Tipping my hard hat to the old girl, I bid her a fond farewell. As I left the area down the mine access road, what was left of Muskie disappeared in a cloud of dust in my rearview mirror.

I called down to the mine in February 2000, to check on the demolition progress on the dragline. Most of Muskie was history by then. Only a few large odds and ends remained, including a good portion of the massive tub. Everything else recognizable had already been hauled off and sold as scrap metal. In the next few months, this would also disappear. The land will be reclaimed and turned into pasture. In a few years, you will not be able to tell that such a monster ever existed. The grazing cows will be none the wiser. But there will be one telltale sign remaining. The massive 220-cubic-yard bucket that was on the machine when it was parked is being preserved as a remembrance to the men and women of Central Ohio Coal and the rich mining legacy of the Cumberland, Ohio, area. It was moved from the mine site in early 2000 to be put on permanent display at a location near McConnelsville, Ohio.

With Big Muskie gone, there are few of the really massive stripping machines left in operation today, especially the shovels. Both of the Bucyrus-Erie 3850-B shovels are gone. Peabody Sinclair Mine's Big Hog was scrapped in 1986, after the Sinclair Mine closed in November 1985. Its sister machine at the River King Mine Number 6 met the same fate in 1993. And the largest shovel of them all, the 180-cubic-yard Marion 6360, was brought to its knees by a fire on September 9, 1991. Deemed too expensive to repair, it was demolished in 1992. At the time of this writing, only two stripping shovels remain in operation: the CONSOL Coal's Bucyrus-Erie 1950-B Silver Spade in Cadiz, Ohio, and a very old Bucyrus-Erie 1050-B model working at Freeman United's Industry Mine, in Industry, Illinois. As were those of their giant relatives, the working days of these machines are surely numbered.

continued on page 126

The rear of Big Muskie shows the earthen ramp leading into the gutted housing of the once-proud machine. Electric motors of various sizes lay around the dragline like evicted tenants, covered up by plastic tarps, in the hopes of finding new homes somewhere else.

The fate of the mighty Marion 6360 stripping shovel is another sad story. Destroyed by fire on September 9, 1991, it was deemed too expensive to repair, sealing its fate. Pictured in July 1992, the 6360 sits silent, waiting for the end to come. By the end of the year, she would be gone.

Not all stories of old giants have unhappy endings. On display in West Mineral, Kansas, is the 90-cubic-yard Bucyrus-Erie 1850-B Brutus shovel, which was owned and operated by Pittsburg & Midway Coal Mining Company. Donated to the nonprofit group of Big Brutus, Inc., it was saved to serve as a monument to the area's rich coal mining heritage. It is shown here in all its glory in August 1998.

Continued from page 122

But all is not lost. You can still see one of these massive shovels in the metal. Located in West Mineral, Kansas, is Pittsburg & Midway (P&M) Coal Mining Company's Bucyrus-Erie 1850-B shovel Brutus. The 90-cubic-yard machine was donated by P&M in 1983 to Big Brutus, Inc., a special nonprofit organization entrusted with the restoration and display of the giant shovel. On July 13, 1985, the shovel was officially dedicated and opened for display. In September 1987, The American Society of Mechanical Engineers (ASME) designated the shovel a regional Historic Mechanical Engineering Landmark, helping to ensure the existence of the machine for decades to come.

While photographing the prototype Liebherr T-282 hauler at the company's Baxter Springs, Kansas, plant for this book, I would take a noontime break and go up to the Big Brutus Museum, which was only about 30 minutes from the Liebherr plant. I would climb all the way to the top of the boom of the shovel and view the surrounding countryside for miles around. That high off the ground, it is very quiet, with just a trace of noise as the wind blows through the hand railings. Coming up from the ground, you can hear the faint sounds of children playing hide and seek between the shovel's massive crawlers. In the distance, just hundreds of rolling green acres . . .

It's strange to think that this was once all coal mining territory. It looks as if it has always been pasture. But that is what reclamation is all about, returning the mined land to its earlier, natural state of being. But if you listen carefully, you can hear the echoes of time, of Brutus' dipper biting into the highwall, and the clapping of its main hoist ropes against each other, like two 2x4s slapped together over your head. They are the memories of mechanical dinosaurs, gone, but not forgotten. Like mighty land-based battleships, their story is one of man's progress and the never-ending quest for energy—the energy that keeps modern society moving ever forward into the future.

BIBLIOGRAPHY

Gowenlock, Philip G. The LeTourneau Legend. Brisbane, Australia: Paddington Publications, 1996.

Learmont, Tom. "A New Dimension in Excavators." Presentation to the 1961 Milwaukee Machine Design Conference.

Learmont, Tom. "Development and Manufacture of a 220 Cubic Yard Walking Dragline." Presentation to the 1967 Coal Convention.

INDEX